Praise for *Teacher-Led I*

Rigorous teacher-led research has much to offer in helping to create an ambitious and accountable self-improving education system. Richard and Eleanor's book offers schools a way to engage in research that is both compelling and deeply worthwhile.

Steve Munby, Chief Executive, Education Development Trust

This volume by Richard Churches and Eleanor Dommett is very carefully crafted to be of use to hardworking, busy teachers. The distinctive feature of the book is its enthusiastic promotion of a scientific approach, drawing on experimental and randomised controlled trial methodologies in particular. The authors' big achievement is to convey the necessary understanding of what can be dry and technical matters with humour and passion.

Ian Menter, Emeritus Professor of Teacher Education, University of Oxford, Former President of the British Educational Research Association

Teacher-Led Research will be of interest to anyone who is involved in practitioner research in schools, or teachers and schools who wish to develop their knowledge and skills in this area and extend their research-based repertoire of tested practical approaches. It contains a wealth of practical examples which are interesting, sometimes even challenging, but then this is exactly the point. Are you brave enough to put your beliefs and assumptions about what is effective to a rigorous test?

Professor Steven Higgins, School of Education, Durham University

Teacher-Led Research gives readers the tools to conduct real research within schools and begin the process of taking a scientific approach to finding out what really works. I'm really impressed with the clarity of *Teacher-Led Research*. It is clear, concise and practical and contains a small library's worth of information. Complex concepts are explained in such a way that they seem easy. What more could you want? Churches and Dommett have distilled the key tools for education research. The impact on teachers and schools could be remarkable.

Paul Kelley, Honorary Clinical Research Associate, Sleep and Circadian Neuroscience Institute (SCNi), University of Oxford

Teacher-Led Research was very useful in consolidating my understanding and gave me a good grounding in what I needed to know before I started my own research. For anyone who is looking to prove that the techniques they are using in the classroom work, this is a great book.

Dave Ashton, Lead Practitioner of Mathematics, Bishop of Llandaff C.I.W. School

This is a great book for teachers and school leaders who are interested in RCTs and want to apply these techniques in their own schools. As well as providing relevant and practical examples, you are encouraged to design and develop your own RCT as you progress through the book's chapters. *Teacher-Led Research* is accessible, well-illustrated and informative – highly recommended for those engaged in, or planning, school-based research.

Dr Jane Doughty CBE, Education Consultant

Teacher-Led Research is more than just a how-to guide for teacher-led research. It offers a pathway for whole school improvement using evidence-based practice. *Teacher-Led Research* allows us to work out not only what does work but, crucially, what doesn't work, so that what we do as practitioners has a positive impact on children's learning.

**James Siddle, Head Teacher, St Margaret's CE Primary School,
Research Lead, Kyra Teaching School Alliance**

Teacher-Led Research will be equally useful to the inexperienced teacher–researcher and the more experienced leader guiding a group. I never thought that I would spend my Saturday evening reading about inferential statistics but found the explanations here much more accessible than in standard texts. Even if you think you have a reasonable understanding, there is much to learn from this book.

Liz Samuel, Head of Sixth Form, The Queen Katherine School

Teacher-Led Research is a very user-friendly book which communicates what could be some rather stuffy maths behind the processes. The book has the appeal of an academic read, but put in an understandable way. It will appeal to the teacher who wants to quantify a 'gut feeling'.

Rob Wilson, Assistant Head Teacher, Llanishen High School

TEACHER-LED
Research

This book is due for return on or before the last date shown below.

Desig   led trials
                                          h

                                          nett

First published by

Crown House Publishing
Crown Buildings,
Bancyfelin,
Carmarthen,
Wales, SA33 5ND, UK
www.crownhouse.co.uk

and

Crown House Publishing Company LLC
6 Trowbridge Drive, Suite 5, Bethel, CT 06801, USA
www.crownhousepublishing.com

British Library Cataloguing-in-Publication Data

A catalogue entry for this book is available from the British Library.

Print ISBN: 978-184590990-1
Mobi ISBN: 978-178583039-6
ePub ISBN: 978-178583040-2
ePDF ISBN: 978-178583041-9

LCCN 2015953355

Printed and bound in the UK by
Bell & Bain Ltd, Thornliebank, Glasgow

Foreword

There was an excitable atmosphere in the packed-out Attlee Suite on the first floor of Portcullis House, the large Gothic Revival parliamentary building adjacent to the Palace of Westminster. None of the utilitarian rooms in Portcullis House, built in 2001, have the gilded finery of the old rooms in the Palace, but this didn't dim the enthusiasm or energy of the occupants on a sunny late spring morning in 2007. Present were a mixture of enlightened parliamentarians, scientists, teachers and representatives from national charities and funding agencies. The occasion was the first public meeting of a pioneering All-Party Parliamentary Group (APPG) that had been recently convened by Baroness Susan Greenfield (Professor of Pharmacology at Oxford University) to debate and promote the importance of scientific research in learning and education. In attendance were stakeholders from many different sectors and backgrounds, united by the common goal to better understand and disseminate best practice in education; to truly understand 'what works'. The meeting marked a milestone in this initiative by building important networks and opening up new lines of communication between sectors.

Attendees included Eleanor, a highly skilled laboratory scientist and lecturer I had known for some years who was just stepping into the world of education policy, and with whom I would later join forces to coordinate the APPG. It was at this meeting that I first met Richard, an enthusiastic former advanced skills teacher, ever-present figure in contemporary education debates and a principal adviser at CfBT Education Trust. In the closing moments of the meeting, Richard raised a vitally important issue upon which the essence of *Teacher-Led Research* is based: that scientists and teachers need to work closely together and learn to use a common language if a rigorous evidence base for what works in education is to be achieved.

In the eight year journey since that first public APPG meeting, much novel research has been undertaken – some examples of which you will find within the pages of this book – and networks between stakeholders have grown in parallel with our understanding of how the best teachers teach. But although much progress has been made there has arguably been negligible impact upon classroom teaching practices. One unavoidable reason for this is that the results from some research studies simply take time to come to fruition. Another reason, however, is the impact of top-down policy decisions and the sweeping changes they can have on teaching priorities, seriously limiting the time available for teachers to engage with research. These changes in policy have occurred unusually frequently since 2007 as a result of three different prime ministers and four ministries. But herein lies the golden opportunity in education research: by collecting evidence for what truly works in the classroom, policies can be rebutted that have no evidential basis and, by working with parliamentarians, new policies launched on the back of sound experimental data. I wholeheartedly agree with the statement of former Education Secretary Baroness Estelle Morris in the 2007 APPG meeting, on the subject of making such changes, that 'the answer has to be to get teachers doing research', but I would go further to suggest that the next part of the journey needs to be led by teachers.

Teacher-Led Research is a unique and timely publication that provides precisely the information necessary to enable teachers to undertake their own classroom research. Richard and Eleanor are ideally suited to this task and have drawn on knowledge built from their classroom experiences, the design and delivery of countless workshops on how to design experiments, their own original research and many years coordinating large collaborative networks in the education sector. Employing a 'practise-what-you-preach' approach, a comprehensive account of how to perform your own classroom experiments is provided in clear, easy-to-understand language in a series of logical steps. Not only is *Teacher-Led Research* an indispensable guide for any teacher wishing to test what teaching practices are most effective, but this book will also tell you how to easily and effectively communicate these findings to your colleagues – a vital additional step in order to contribute to a growing national body of work.

Dr Ian Devonshire, PhD, CSci, FRSA, Nottingham University Medical School

Preface

40,000 Faradays – new directions for education research

This book begins with high hopes and even greater aspirations. As we write this, the first 100 teacher-led research projects employing scientific method are concluding. Many of these are taking place in teaching schools in England (an initiative that began in 2010/2011 with the aim of paralleling the role of teaching hospitals in medicine – institutions where high quality research underpins outstanding training and patient outcomes in a way that models best practice for the system as a whole). Teachers in Wales and Dubai have also successfully shown that  they can lead research using scientific methods, analysing and interpreting results with skill and accuracy, as evidenced in the publication, *Evidence That Counts – What Happens When Teachers Apply Scientific Methods To Their Practice*.[1]

The journey to this point has developed from collaborative work between scientists and teachers through to teacher-led initiatives. Both Richard and Eleanor (with Ian Devonshire) were involved in one of the first educational studies to use experimental research in England – a project led by Susan Greenfield and funded by the CfBT Education Trust (now the Education Development Trust) that began in 2009. Back then things were very different, and engaging and explaining scientific method and experimental research to teachers was much more time consuming as they had few frames of reference to draw upon. Nonetheless, the teachers' enthusiasm carried the three-year project through to its final successful conclusion.[2] The project fed into the House of Lords All-Party Parliamentary Group on Scientific Research in Learning and Education and featured as part of an event on Neuroscience in the Classroom at the British Science Festival in 2013.

Through these various initiatives, and over many years, it has become clear that teachers have a great appetite for learning about experimental research design, and the desire to use such methods both to conduct their own publishable research and as a tool in achieving school improvement – a

---

1   R. Churches and T. McAleavy, *Evidence That Counts – What Happens When Teachers Apply Scientific Methods To Their Practice: Twelve Teacher-Led Randomised Controlled Trials and Other Styles of Experimental Research* (Reading: CfBT Education Trust, 2015). Available at: https://www.educationdevelopmenttrust.com

2   E. Dommett, I. M. Devonshire, E. Sewter and S. A. Greenfield, 'The impact of participation in a neuroscience course on motivational measures and academic performance', *Trends in Neuroscience and Education* 2(3–4) (2013): 122–138.

fact evidenced by the successful work of the Education Endowment Foundation in England and the wide range of randomised controlled trials that have taken place around the world in recent years.[3]

The original project in 2009 worked with teachers on a study designed by scientists but over the years the dynamics have changed. Now teachers design and run their own studies. This approach began with Closing the Gap: Test and Learn, a Department for Education and National College for Teaching and Leadership programme which pooled 200 teaching schools together with 700 other schools to collaborate on the design and implementation of education research using scientific method.[4] As part of this programme, Richard travelled around England training teachers in how to implement this kind of research. He effectively taught them the kind of introduction to experimental research design that would be taught to psychology students, with no greater intention than helping teachers to get an understanding of this style of research.

Within a few weeks, a teacher in the north-west of England (Liz Samuel) conducted the first experimental study with her A level students. From this initial study enthusiasm grew within the group of teachers. It soon became apparent that with training in scientific method, teachers could conduct their own research into areas of particular interest in their classrooms, taking control of education research and putting it at the front line, so to speak.

This is what happens when people learn about scientific method. Indeed, if we look back at the history of science and how scientific understanding of the natural world developed, it is not a history of large pharmaceutical companies, research grants or even necessarily university-led research (although often people who conducted studies had learned their skills within a university). Rather, the history of science is littered with the stories of enthusiasts who, applying a controlled scientific approach to a problem, discovered amazing things. Because they then shared their findings by writing up what they did, others could replicate their findings by doing the experiment again, so that scientific method and knowledge grew fast and in a way that was unstoppable.

Take Faraday, for example. Michael Faraday (1791–1867) had very little in the way formal education, yet he ended up as one of the most important and influential researchers in the history of science. Among his many achievements was establishing the basis for the theory and practice around electromagnetism, ideas and concepts that largely remain in place today, despite many years of further enquiry. What enabled Faraday to achieve this was method; using scientific method to be precise. This was combined with clear and straightforward experiments and the ability to communicate them in a way that made it easy for others to replicate his findings and build on his theories. If only 10% of teachers in England engaged in experimental research in this way, we could have 40,000 Faradays in education. Even if they produced only one important piece of trial evidence in their career, the effect and potential for replication could be truly transformational.

---

3   Professor Paul Connolly's forthcoming literature review (previewed at the 2015 British Educational Research Association conference) indicates well over 800 university-associated RCTs have been conducted over the last 10 years.
4   The inclusion of experimental research training in this programme would not have happened without the innovative and forward thinking of Juliet Brookes and Robin Hall.

Randomised controlled trials in education

As we write this book, there is no doubt that evidence has come of age within the teaching profession. As a UK Cabinet Office paper, commenting on a particular type of experimental approach, put it in 2012, 'Randomised controlled trials (RCTs) are the best way of determining whether a policy is working.'[5]

At the same time, the notion of the importance of teacher-generated school-based research is also centre stage. In many ways, saying this seems like an extraordinary statement, implying what is simply not the case – namely, that teachers and other education and public sector professionals have not been as diligent as they could have been. This, of course, is far from the truth. In fact, as Haynes et al. also note, if we look at evidence-based practice outside of teaching and in the wider public sector, it is instantly clear that this shift has occurred across a wide range of areas of public policy only recently. Indeed, the number of randomised controlled trials that have taken place in the areas of health, social welfare, education and crime and justice rose exponentially from virtually none between 1900 and 1959 (with only a modest number in the 1960s) to nearly 200,000 in the 1990s.[6] This said, few of these were education related (unless conducted within the sphere of educational psychology). Thus, the change in thinking that has taken place in recent years within schools and education departments is in many ways a reflection of wider demands and a sort of 'catch up' on the part of those of us engaged in working with schools.

It is not, however, the place of this book to spend too much time debating or recording the history and development of the evidence movement in education. There are many other excellent discussions that explore the nature of being evidence-based or not – for those interested, we highly recommend Tony McAleavy's publication, *Teaching As a Research-Engaged Profession*.[7]

Rather, this book is intended to be a 'how-to' guide for those already convinced by the arguments and debates, whether they use the term evidence-based, evidence-informed, evidence-engaged or evidence-led to describe the way they now think about the challenge of making a difference to the learners they teach. This book is therefore for people like us and the teachers we have worked with over the last few years – teachers who believe in and want to design research in their own schools and the schools they are associated with – research which taps in to the long history of scientific method and what it offers.

At the same time, it is important to recognise that a complex field of study such as education needs more than a simple reductionist approach. Therefore, at no point are we arguing for a shift to the exclusive use of the style of research we describe. Indeed, some education research questions would

---

5   L. Haynes, O. Service, B. Goldacre and D. Torgerson, *Test, Learn, Adapt: Developing Public Policy with Randomised Controlled Trials* (London: Cabinet Office, 2012). Available at: https://www.gov.uk/government/uploads/system/uploads/attachment_data/file/62529/TLA-1906126.pdf, p. 6.

6   J. Shepherd, 'The production and management of evidence for public service reform', *Evidence and Policy* 3(2) (2007): 231–251.

7   T. McAleavy, *Teaching As a Research-Engaged Profession: Problems and Possibilities* (Reading: CfBT Education Trust, 2015). Available at: https://www.educationdevelopmenttrust.com

not be effectively answered in this way. Nevertheless, and we hope that this is now the case, perhaps people in the field of education can feel more comfortable in realising the value of experimental research design as part of a mixed methodology.

Getting the most out of this book

Although we have organised the book so you can dip in and out of it, we recommend that you read it from cover to cover in the first instance, completing the various activities as you go along. The reason for this is that each chapter builds on the next.

Alongside the main narrative, the book has the following features:

- *Glossary terms* – All words and phrases that are key subject knowledge are indicated in **bold** the first time they appear. These terms can be found in the glossary at the end of the book.

- *Brain boxes* – These text boxes contain additional explanations, extended ideas or descriptions.

- *Learning zones* – These are short boxed sections that include a task to enhance your understanding.

- *Test yourself* – At the end of each chapter there are self-assessment questions that will help you to review your knowledge and remind yourself of the main topics that you have learned in the preceding section. You can find the answers to these questions at the end of the book.

Contents

Contents

List of figures

List of tables

Chapter 1
An introduction to scientific method

By the end of this chapter, you will know about:

- The stages of scientific method.
- The difference between experimental and observational research.
- Research ethics.

Scientific method

Scientific method is the name given to a process of designing and conducting research that involves making observations and interpreting them in the context of very specific questions. It is not a new method. Indeed, there is even a reference to such an experiment in the Bible to examine the impact of eating meat and wine compared to a vegetarian diet with no alcohol:

> But Daniel appealed to a steward who had been assigned by the head of the palace staff to be in charge of Daniel, Hananiah, Mishael, and Azariah. 'Try us out for ten days on a simple diet of vegetables and water. Then compare us with the young men who eat from the royal menu. Make your decision on the basis of what you see.' The steward agreed to do it and fed them vegetables and water for ten days. At the end of the ten days they looked better and more robust than all the others who had been eating from the royal menu.

> **Daniel 1: 11–14**

While this biblical reference illustrates that the process is not new, it does not tell us much about how it works beyond the central importance of comparing different conditions. In this case the two 'conditions' are two types of diet. This detail is best illustrated with a flow chart showing the process step by step (see Figure 1.1).

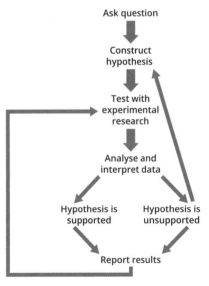

Figure 1.1. Scientific method begins with a specific question.

As you can see, the process of scientific method begins with a specific question. There is nothing special about this question – it will often have arisen through curiosity or some attempt to explain a previous observation.

Let's take a very simple example and ask the question, 'Why are carrots orange?' Once we have asked the question, we might attempt to find some information to help us answer it. This information could be reports from previous research or it could be the opinions of experts on colour pigments. In a classroom context, teachers views based on professional experience might be the starting point.

After we have collected some background information about how this could be measured, we need to construct a **hypothesis**. A hypothesis is a formal statement of what we think the answer to the question might be. In this case the hypothesis may be:

> Carrots are orange because they contain the pigment carotene.

This is a statement that we can test (assuming we had access to carrots and a lab!). Importantly, the hypothesis needs to be a statement that the outcome of the experimental research could support (i.e. agree with) or not support (i.e. disagree with). Once we have completed the test and interpreted the results, in the context of the original hypothesis, the results are then reported somewhere for others to read. We can then continue the process by revising our hypothesis if the results did not support our original hypothesis or attempting to replicate our findings if they did support it.

Replication means repeating a study in order to see if the same result occurs again. As you will learn later, we are only ever dealing with probabilities in this type of research. Specifically, our findings are all related to the probability that the result may have happened by chance, so there is always the possibility that we may be wrong. Replication helps to solve this problem because if the result is true, we are likely to find it repeated more times than not.

Remember: we are only ever dealing with probabilities in this type of research. Replication helps to solve this problem.

Of course, in this simplified example the process looks quite straightforward, so you may find it hard to see how scientific method, when described in this way, can be applied to complex contexts such as education, which will clearly require more complex experimental research than that required for testing for the presence of a particular pigment in a carrot. In order to see how this can be done, it is necessary to explain a little more about the concept of experimental research. Before we do this, you may want to complete the activity in Learning Zone 1.1 so that you have some ideas to play with later on.

Learning Zone 1.1. What would you like to find out?

Think about a topic you are interested in exploring and try to come up with some questions on which you could base some research. Here are a few ideas to get you started.

- Which is better for learning times tables – rote learning or flash cards?
- What is the effect of group work on reducing misconceptions in column addition?
- Do girls or boys perform better when given structured homework compared to a freer approach?
- Does an intervention you are thinking of using (which is shown to be effective in another context) work in your own school?

Approaches to research

Now that you have some questions of interest, let's look more carefully at what is meant by experimental research. The term 'experimental' is banded around quite freely so most people have a general idea of what it means. If we think of something as experimental we are recognising that the outcome, whether it is taking a drug or trying a new hair style, is somewhat unknown. This is also true of the term when it is used in the context of research; however, here it takes on a rather more specific meaning.

Experimental research refers to a type of investigation that uses the manipulation of **variables** (or things of interest) and controlled testing to understand causal events. Although this sounds complex, it is easy to understand if we compare experimental research to another type of research – **observational research**. In observational research, the researcher observes participants and measures variables without controlling for other factors or directly allocating people to certain conditions. For example, if a researcher is interested in the effect of multivitamins on self-esteem in women, this could be studied using experimental research or observational research. Table 1.1 illustrates the different approaches.

Experimental	Observational
Find 100 women who do not currently take any vitamins and have 'average' or 'normal' levels of self-esteem.	Find 100 women, 50 of whom have been taking multivitamins for three months.
Randomly allocate 50 women to a group in which they must take multivitamins and 50 to a group where they must not take multivitamins.	
Measure self-esteem after the women have been in the conditions for three months.	Measure self-esteem in these women.
Analyse and interpret the data.	Analyse and interpret the data.

Table 1.1. The difference between experimental and observational research.

For the experimental research approach, you can see that the researcher directly manipulates the variable of vitamin intake by placing some participants in one condition (where they receive vitamins) and others in a different condition (where they do not receive vitamins). By doing this, the researcher is able to examine causality between two things (multivitamins and self-esteem) rather than simply associations between the two things. There is, however, no such manipulation for the observational version of the study.

In education, until recently, we have tended to take an observational approach without comparing our intervention to something else at the same time (such as a control condition) – a practice that generally means we have never been entirely sure whether the change might have happened anyway.

Types of experimental research

Experimental research typically involves some form of **randomisation** to different groups before exposing them to a treatment or a control (see Figure 1.2). It is also possible to collect both quantitative and qualitative research data during this process.

In this way, studies could be seen as fitting into one of the four quadrants in Figure 1.3.

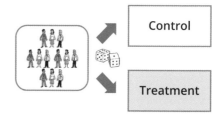

Figure 1.2. A typical piece of experimental research.

	Experimental	Observational
Quantitative	Manipulation of the area being explored by creating comparison conditions Numerical data	No manipulation Numerical data
Qualitative	Manipulation of the area being explored by creating comparison conditions Other forms of data	No manipulation Other forms of data

Figure 1.3. Types of research.

Qualitative research refers to research using methods that provide information about the 'human' or personal side of the issue or subject being investigated – for example, information about beliefs, opinions and subjective responses to situations. It typically employs open-ended questions in semi-structured interviews. This information is not quantified or turned into numbers, but rather may exist as text or transcript from interviews.

By contrast, **quantitative research** tends to work with fixed scales, closed questions and aspects that can be objectively measured, such as body temperature. These data exist as numbers which then allows for complex statistical analysis. For example, where a piece of experimental quantitative research might randomise patients into a group for treatment (comparing this to a control group) and then measure how many patients were cured as a result of the treatment, a piece of experimental qualitative design might follow the same sort of randomisation process but then collect semi-structured interview data. In a school context, you could randomly allocate classes to different forms of pedagogy and then collect similar data.

As a teacher or school leader, the types of effectiveness that you will probably be interested in measuring will include things like attainment, progress, behaviour, attendance and maybe aspects of engagement, confidence and pupil well-being. Some of these may be best measured qualitatively and others quantitatively.

Using quantitative research in the best way

Quantitative experimental research is not always the most effective way to answer a research question. It is best deployed when you want to compare one thing with another and see which one is better according to a particular test or numerical scale. In other words, you need to have something in mind that you want to test the effectiveness of, either against a control condition (such as normal practice) or against another intervention, or perhaps with regard to the responses of different groups when they are exposed to the same intervention.

By contrast, quantitative experimental research is not very good at more generally exploring or answering questions that require you to figure out what something means to a group of people. For example, if you wanted to find out about the experience of newly qualified teachers in New Zealand or the impact of a new teaching approach, you would need to use a different form of research – for example, qualitative research or an observational study. You might even need to embed yourself in the context as a participant observer and do ethnographic education research.

Advantages and disadvantages of quantitative experimental research

The advantages of using quantitative experimental research design can be summarised as follows:

- It can be much more objective than other forms of research, and providing the measures used are valid and reliable there is less risk of misinterpretation.
- Replication can remove the risk of the falsification of results or of findings that are unusual and unlikely to occur again.
- As the analytical approach is statistical, there is the potential for in-depth understanding of the characteristics that underpin the findings and for later **meta-analysis** (the combining of evidence from a wide range of studies of the same topic in order to make some robust generalisations about the effects of a treatment in the real world).
- Collecting the data you need and the initial analysis of what you have found can be much faster – depending on your research design.
- It is possible to recommend a future study that builds on your design in a way that can further validate and confirm your findings in an objective way.

The disadvantages of using quantitative experimental research design can be summarised as follows:

- Quantitative experimental research is not good at telling you why something is happening, and in the end it still requires interpretation – taking into account the context and the circumstances in which the experiment took place.

- It cannot elicit complex ideas about the way people perceive things to be or their understanding of a situation.
- It only tells you something about the thing you have measured and only whether one thing is different to another. It is quite possible that something important has gone on which you have not measured, so you must always consider this when writing up.

There are many different ways of conducting experimental research and we do not have time to discuss them all here. Rather, this book is concerned with quantitative experimental research only. If you are interested in learning about a wider range of research methods, we highly recommend:

Ian Menter, Dely Elliot, Moira Hulme, Jon Lewin and Kevin Lowden, *A Guide to Practitioner Research in Education* (London: SAGE, 2011).

Learning Zone 1.2. To experiment or not to experiment? That is the question ...

Take each of the ideas that you generated in Learning Zone 1.1 and consider them in the light of the advantages and disadvantages of using quantitative experimental research. Then decide on which of the approaches might be best:

- Experimental or observational research.
- Quantitative or qualitative design.

Make sure you have at least one idea that you think you can test with quantitative experimental research, as this will be the focus of the remainder of this book and we will be asking you to plan a research study as you improve your understanding.

Research ethics

Before we move on to look at how you conduct research in more detail, it is important to be aware of the ethical implications of your work. If the research is a drug trial for a particular medical condition or a psychological experiment investigating a sensitive issue, it is easy to see why ethics are important. However, the same considerations are necessary in classroom research because any form of research that involves people is not without 'risk of harm'. This can take different forms and can range from a risk of physical harm (e.g. when a participant takes part in a study on sports) to a risk of psychological harm (e.g. when a participant is subjected to psychological stress, such as through additional school tests).

Privacy and data protection

An important aspect of research is the protection of the participants' privacy. It is important that test results are not shared with the rest of the world in such a manner that individuals can be identified. Data should be anonymised in some way so that each participant in the study gets a unique identification number and their test data is stored under this ID number rather than under their name or other identifiable feature. In this way, people outside the research group cannot identify an individual. Within the UK, researchers must also comply with the Data Protection Act 1998.

Getting approval

In addition to legal requirements, research normally needs to be approved by an independent ethics committee before it can take place. The ethics committee will look at a detailed plan of the research and do a cost benefit analysis to see if it can be justified. In a school, the head teacher and/or the governing body are generally the equivalent. However, if you are doing your research as part of an MA, MED, MSc or PhD, you may need to engage with both the school's senior leadership and your university. Once approved, the researcher should carry out the work exactly as they have planned.

Informed consent

When carrying out the research, it is important that consent is obtained from the participants. This is not simply them verbally saying yes or turning up for your study; the consent cannot be implied or informal. In fact, the type of consent required from your participants is called **informed consent**. To obtain this, each participant must be informed about the aims of the study, what it will actually involve and what you believe the benefits and risks to be. This is the *informed* part of the consent.

Normally, you would provide participants with an **information sheet** which would specify these details and which they would be required to read. This sheet is normally part of the research detail that is approved by the ethics committee. After each participant has read the information sheet and you have answered any questions they may have, they must formally give their *consent*. Similar to the information sheet, the written consent is not simply an empty piece of paper, but a standard 'informed consent form' that the ethics committee will have approved. Note that when a participant is under 18 years of age you must have consent from a parent or guardian for their participation, and this individual has the right to see the data from a child in their care if they request it. It is important to note that the participant has the right to withdraw from the study at any point, including after their data has been collected, and they must be made aware of this (it is normally covered on the information sheet). If participants withdraw, their data must be removed or destroyed.

Learning Zone 1.3. Finding out what people say about the question of ethics

We recommend extending your thinking about how, and within what ethical framework, to apply a psychological experimental method within an education setting. To do this you may want to read the code of ethics that the American Psychological Association and British Psychological Association have produced. These can be found at the following websites, where there are specific sections relating to the protection of research participants:

www.apa.org

www.bps.org.uk

The British Educational Research Association (BERA) also has a research ethics publication which is available at:

www.bera.ac.uk

Test yourself 1

Question 1

Why is replication important in scientific method?

Question 2

A researcher, interested in the impact of caffeinated drinks at lunchtime on afternoon concentration levels, decides to measure attainment in 30 children who have routinely drunk caffeinated drinks and 30 who have not. Is this an experimental or observational study?

Question 3

Identify two advantages and two disadvantages of quantitative research.

What next?

Now that you have learned about what is meant by scientific method and experimental research, we will move on to the first stage of carrying out this kind of research. This involves turning your research question into a hypothesis. To do this, you need to make some decisions about what exactly you will manipulate and measure. These considerations are the focus of the next chapter.

Chapter 2

From research question to hypothesis

By the end of this chapter, you will know about:

- How to write a research aim.
- Independent and dependent variables.
- Confounding and extraneous variables.

Perfecting your research question

You will recall that the first stage of scientific method is to ask a question. The point of this is to have a clear goal that you want to achieve. We will use the term **research aim** from now on, as it is has a good metaphor associated with it.

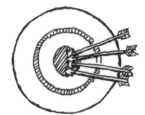

Being able to state your research aim early in your planning, and later when you come to implement your study, is a very good thing. It gives you a benchmark to look back on when you decide on the measures that you will use and if the approaches you are taking are valid and reliable. Think of your research aim as the centre of a target and visualise what it is that you want to find out (see Figure 2.1). If your study is going to be effective, each arrow you fire (e.g. the recruitment of participants, the intervention you have designed, the measures that you use) needs to hit the centre of the target and be aligned to your research aim.

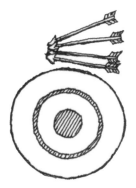

The simplest and most practical way to phrase your research aim is to use a sentence structure that begins, 'To find out whether …' For example, a study could have two research aims:

> To find out whether modelling maths problems from the very start of a lesson improves attainment for lower performing pupils.

> To find out whether modelling maths problems from the very start of a lesson improves enjoyment for lower performing pupils.

Figure 2.1. Is your research on target to achieve your research aim (or objective)?

Notice how in this example, we have a separate aim for each thing that needs to be measured. Adopting this approach makes it easier to keep track of the different testing you are going to have to apply.

Learning Zone 2.1. Create some research aims

Think back to a research question that you devised in Chapter 1.

Ask yourself:

- What is important in this study in terms of what I want to find out?
- How many of these types of things are there?

Make a list of the important things, then decide which ones you want to focus on – these should be types of things that you can measure in some way (e.g. attainment, well-being according to a well-being scale, attendance or exclusion rates).

Now, try to phrase it as a research aim, like the examples we gave above. Here is another example to get you going.

> To find out whether three lessons of group work improves English creative essay writing marks.

Once you have your research aim, you need to operationalise this to create a hypothesis. As we discussed, your hypothesis needs to be written as a testable statement. It should also refer to two types of variable within your experiment – the thing you manipulate and the thing you measure. In order for you to understand how this works we first need to explain some core concepts.

Independent variables and dependent variables – thinking like a scientist

There are two key types of variable in your experiment. The first one we will look at in detail is the **independent variable (IV)**, which is the thing you manipulate. The second one is the **dependent variable (DV)**, which is the thing you measure.

Independent variables

As stated above, the independent variable is the thing that you manipulate in your experiment. It is what you input into the experiment (usually the treatment or intervention that you are interested in exploring) (see Figure 2.2).

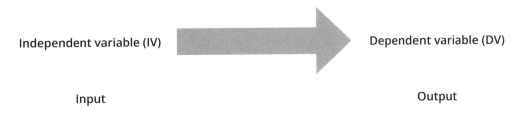

Figure 2.2. The independent variable is the input and the dependent variable is the output.

The number of different things that you trial at once (the conditions) are called the **levels** of the independent variable. For example, if you were interested in looking at the impact of working group size on column addition problem-solving, your independent variable would be 'group size'. If you decided to test 'working in groups of three' (trios) against normal classroom practice (working alone), there would be two levels to your independent variable:

IV level 1 (control condition) – Normal classroom practice (working alone)

IV level 2 (experimental condition (or intervention)) – Trio groups

Your dependent variable would be a measure of the children's column addition problem-solving.

As we will see later, it is perfectly possible to have more than two levels to your independent variable. For example, in relation to the example above, you might want to include a third level – perhaps adding 'paired working'.

IV level 1 – Normal classroom practice (working alone)

IV level 2 – Trio groups

IV level 3 – Paired working

In other words, you would expose the children in your study to three different classroom experiences.

Naturally occurring levels of your independent variable

There are, of course, instances when the independent variable you are interested in cannot be manipulated. The most common of these might occur in education if you wanted to find out whether there was a difference in attainment between boys and girls in response to the same treatment. Here, the input into the experiment (the IV) would be 'gender'.

We apply the term **quasi-experiment** to such situations. We do this because, although the study will follow all the other conventions of experimental research, the independent variable cannot be manipulated.

A classic quasi-experimental design from psychology

It is well-established that an aspect of personality type influences your heart rate in response to stress. This was discovered by giving people a questionnaire to first establish if they were a type A or type B personality.[1] Basically, if you find yourself in the queue at the post office – like Richard did waiting to send his passport to a visa office – and you find yourself getting quite agitated, you are probably a type A personality. However, if – like Richard's dad – you see queuing as an opportunity to take a break and chill out from the daily routine, you are probably a type B personality.

In the research design (see Figure 2.3), once participants' personality types were clear, they were put into one of two research groups (A or B as appropriate). Then both groups were exposed to the same treatment (in this case, a period of stressful activity – working under a time pressure to crack a problem that could not be solved). Here the independent variable is personality type and the levels are type A or type B. Following exposure to the same treatment, they both have their heart rate measured (the output and therefore the dependent variable).

You might need to use the same design in education if, for example, you wanted to see whether boys and girls respond differently to independent learning tasks embedded in a particular scheme of work (see Figure 2.4).

---

1   C. A. Essau and J. L. Jamieson, 'Heart rate perception in the type A personality', *Health Psychology* 6(1) (1987): 43–54.

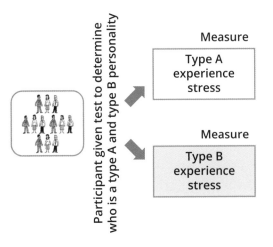

Figure 2.3. A classic quasi-experimental design to assess the effect of exposure to stress on personality type.

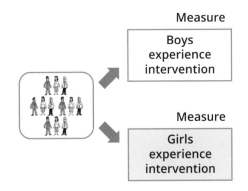

Figure 2.4. A quasi-experimental design in which both boys and girls have been exposed to the same treatment.

Dependent variables

As we have just established, what you decide to measure (in order to assess the effects of the different levels of IV) is called the dependent variable. Your test or measure is called the dependent variable because it is what depends on your manipulation of the IV. For the maths column addition example we gave previously, the dependent variable might be a 30-problem 10-minute test.

You can have more than one dependent variable in a study. For example, you might want to assess student confidence in response to the different conditions that you have exposed them to as well as attainment. Brain Box 2.1 gives you an example of how you might technically describe this study if it just had two levels to the IV.

Brain Box 2.1. Technical descriptions of your independent variables and dependent variables

Here is an example of the way you might write about your independent variables and dependent variables when doing a research plan for your study.

The independent variable 'group work' will be operationally defined by creating two conditions:

IV level 1 (control condition) – Normal classroom practice, involving a mixture of whole class, individual and paired working

IV level 2 (experimental condition) – Trio groups in which children sit in groups of three at cafe style tables and work collaboratively for the whole lesson

There will be two dependent variables:

DV1 – Average score on a 30-item 10-minute test

DV2 – Student confidence in doing column addition measured by giving the children a post-lesson questionnaire

The term 'operational definition' refers to the way in which we decide to construct an experiment in order to measure the effects of that experiment. In the example above, we have operationally defined both the independent and the dependent variables.

The validity and reliability of your dependent variable

When deciding on what you will measure you need to consider the validity and reliability of your proposed dependent variable. There are many different types of validity and reliability (see Brain Box 2.2). All of these, broadly speaking, ask the same question: is the dependent variable you have chosen fit for purpose? We will deal with validity first and then go on to talk about reliability.

If you are interested in the effect of different maths teaching approaches on attainment, it would be foolish to choose to measure those effects with a test of literacy comprehension, wouldn't it? In this situation, we would say that the measure was lacking validity. Of course, this is a rather simplistic example. However, it is not unusual for this basic mistake to be made in a more subtle way, resulting in the adoption of what is sometimes referred to as a **surrogate measure**.

A surrogate measure is a dependent variable that is effectively a proxy for the area that you are interested in measuring. Sometimes a surrogate measure can be useful as a way of adding in additional information to help you interpret your findings. However, you should avoid using surrogate measures just because what you are interested in measuring is difficult to test. If you find yourself in this situation, look to see if someone else has measured the area before and question if a quantitative experimental approach is the right one.

A good example of a surrogate measure in education might be measuring the effect of a leadership development programme by looking at attainment in physics lessons. Although student attainment is probably mediated by the quality of the school's leadership (i.e. unhappy teachers probably don't teach as well), this is not a direct relationship as many good teachers might continue to teach well despite the quality of leadership in the school. In this situation, a 360-degree quantitative leadership feedback tool would probably be a better choice.

The second thing you need to consider is whether your dependent variable is reliable – that is, if you were to repeat the test or questionnaire, is it likely to produce the same results for the same group of children or for different ones? The notions of validity and reliability with regard to a dependent variable are often summarised in diagrams like Figure 2.5, which illustrates the four possible scenarios of either having validity and reliability or not.

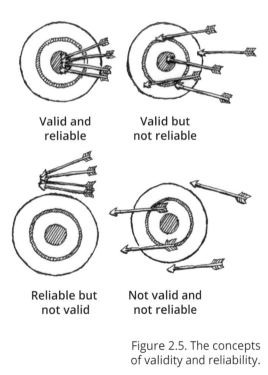

Valid and reliable

Valid but not reliable

Reliable but not valid

Not valid and not reliable

Figure 2.5. The concepts of validity and reliability.

As a final example, suppose your aim was:

> To find out whether visualisation improves performance in a PE lesson where the focus is the basketball penalty shoot.

Not an unreasonable research aim, bearing in mind that there is evidence from a range of experimental psychology studies suggesting that such things may improve performance with professional sports people. Yet so far, even though some GCSE syllabuses include the idea, no studies have taken place into children's performance.

You might decide to define your main dependent variable (DV1) like this:

> DV1 – Mean scores from throwing 10 baskets and counting the number of successful throws

And perhaps adopting as a second dependent variable:

> DV2 – The number of baskets scored with the first throw

Collecting both these measures would make your design more efficient and, if the visualisation took place immediately prior to throwing the ball, deals with the issue of the potential effects of visualisation wearing off as the children progress from throw 1 to 10.

Brain Box 2.2. Types of validity and reliability

Getting your test to work correctly has long been a topic of considerable debate and research. Those of you who are intending to do research at postgraduate level will want to do some additional reading in this area. To start you off, below is a description of the main types of validity and reliability that are considered important. Which ones are most important with regard to a particular test will depend on what it is trying to do, the participants and the nature of your independent variable.

- Construct validity – The extent to which the measure reflects the concept that it is intending to measure. This is often assessed using factor analysis – a form of data reduction to investigate whether a larger set of variables (e.g. a long list of personality traits) are related to a smaller set of variables (e.g. a list of summary categories).

- Concurrent validity – If you compared the test with another measure at the sample point in time and that other measure (or criterion) is based on a related construct, whether the two tests are associated with each other statistically (i.e. whether they produce similar results).

- Convergent validity – This is the degree of association between two tests that you assume measure the same thing.

- Discriminant validity – This is the opposite of convergent validity. In other words, the extent to which two measures, presumed to assess different concepts, lack association as expected.
- Inter-rater reliability – This is the extent to which two observers of the same behaviour would agree if they used the same method of assessment.
- Internal consistency reliability – You can do tests on a questionnaire to check that, where a number of items contribute to a single concept, these items correlate with each other. If they do, then the questionnaire is considered to have internal consistency reliability. The test commonly used is called Cronbach's alpha.
- Predictive validity – The assessment of whether a test predicts scores on a related measure or suitable concept.
- Test–retest reliability – If the test responses are stable when they are repeated at two different points in time.

Range, ceiling and floor effects

A final and important thing to consider in relation to your dependent variable is the extent to which it has a wide enough range to detect an effect and avoid ceiling and floor effects.

A **ceiling effect** occurs when participants are too easily able to score the highest mark on a test, resulting in the true extent of their understanding or attainment being masked by the nature of the test itself. A **floor effect** occurs if the test may not extend low enough with regard to attainment, resulting in an artificial amplification of the true nature of the participants' abilities.

Brain Box 2.3. The Likert scale – a really great tool!

As well as using classroom tests (and maybe even standardised tests that you have purchased as your dependent variable), you may also want to operationally define more subjective concepts, such as happiness. A Likert scale is a great way to do this and consists of a statement that the participants rate their own view against. For example:

I feel very happy with my progress

Disagree   1   2   3   4   5   6   7   Agree

Alternatively, you could have two opposing statements at each end of the scale.

I am not at all happy   1   2   3   4   5   6   7   I am completely happy

In terms of range of scale, it is better to have lots of steps in your scale as then the scale will be more sensitive to small changes. Related to this point is another issue: if you have an even number of scale points (e.g. 6) you are going to force the data to be skewed because there won't be a middle option. This could reduce your choices when you analyse the data (as you will learn in Chapter 5). As a rule of thumb, unless you have a very good reason to use a 6-point scale, then go for 7. This is a moot point when it comes to many classroom attainment tests as these are going to end up yielding marks out of 10 to 100 so there is no real issue.

Types of data

Your dependent variable could consist of different types of measure. There are three different types of data you can collect: interval, ordinal and nominal (or categorical). **Interval data** is what you might think of as 'real' data, like height, reaction time, maths scores and so on. The key feature of this type of data is that you can assess the size of the differences between measurements. For example, if three participants had a maths score of 24%, 38% and 70% respectively, then you can meaningfully say that the difference in score between the first two (14%) is smaller than the difference between the last two (32%). This is probably the most likely form your dependent variable will take.

For **ordinal data** it is possible to say that one number is larger than another but not to assess the size of the differences. This is the kind of data collected from a Likert scale. For example, you may be able to assess the extent of interpersonal contact with peers in the presence of their normal teacher or a new teacher using a rating scale:

1. No contact ☐   2. Occasional contact ☐   3. Frequent contact ☑   4. Constant contact ☐

It would be possible to assign any contact under investigation to one or other of four points on the scale. Hence, you could rank contact in different experimental conditions (i.e. presence or absence of a new teacher) and say that contact at point 2 was less than at point 4. Here, though, it would not be meaningful to say that the difference between points 1 and 2 contact is any larger or smaller than the difference between points 3 and 4 contact.

Finally, **nominal data** (also known as categorical data) allows you to say that someone or something belongs to a particular category but you cannot rank the categories. An example in an education context might be the number of pupils who sign up for GCSE history at the end of Year 9 in one year compared to another year.

Brain Box 2.3. How one teacher incorporated several different dependent variables in a study on handwriting improvement

One teacher in England, who completed a study with funding from the Department for Education/National College for Teaching and Leadership Closing the Gap: Test and Learn programme (Frances Bryant-Khachy), looked at the effects of a particular intervention on children's ability to write more effectively.[2] Her independent variable was playing darts (the game). She created two levels within her between-participant design:

> IV level 1 (control condition) – No darts throwing in the morning

> IV level 2 (intervention) – Darts throwing in the morning

She got young children in the experimental group to throw darts three mornings a week and had a control group who did no darts throwing. In order to explore the effects of the intervention (darts throwing) she decided to have more than one dependent variable, as below:

> DV1 – The number of words that children could write in ten minutes (as a measure of fluency)

> DV2 – Children's self-reported discomfort on a Likert scale following the writing test (as a measure of whether the intervention had reduced the discomfort young children often have in response to holding a pen and writing in an extended way)

> DV 3 – Standard or non-standard pen gripping (measured by taking photographs of the pupils' writing hands as they wrote and making a judgement on the quality of their grip)

This study nicely illustrates that you can have a range of different types of data in one piece of research. Her first dependent variable is interval data, the second is ordinal and the third is nominal (or categorical).

Secondary dependent variables

So far we have talked about what we call **primary data**. Primary data comes from measures that you deliberately insert into your research. However, you can also use **secondary data** as a dependent variable. This is data that you already collect as part of your everyday school improvement processes. Such measures include things like attendance rate, punctuality rate, exclusion days, effort grades and teacher grades that are part of a formal school assessment system.

---

2   Thanks to Frances Bryant-Khachy for letting us quote her research design in our book.

Learning Zone 2.2. Identifying your independent and dependent variables

Go back to the research aims that you generated for some research studies in Learning Zone 2.1 and take a few moments to think about each one and the practicalities of delivering it in your own school context. Then answer the following questions for each one:

1   What is your independent variable, and what are the levels of your independent variable?

2   What dependent variable(s) will you use to compare the effects of the different levels of the independent variable?

3   Will you be able to manipulate the independent variable (i.e. allocate participants to the levels of the IV), or is this a quasi-experiment?

Other variables to consider

Conducting your research well requires you to do more than just think about your dependent and independent variables. You also need to give some thought to all the other variables that might affect your design. These other variables fit into two categories: confounding variables and extraneous variables.

A **confounding variable** is something that varies with your independent variable. Imagine that you decided to test the effects of a problem-based learning approach. If you had all the pupils with poor attendance in the experimental condition and all the 100% attending pupils in the experimental condition, you would not be able to tell if any differences you found between the levels of the independent variable were due to your problem-based approach or to attendance. In this case, you risk attendance 'confounding' your findings. Other examples could include:

• Sustained noise outside the classroom that is overly distracting in one condition but not the other.

• Very different classroom layouts, if they impact on the type of classroom pedagogy you are testing.

• Wide variations in the way the teachers apply what you have planned for the control condition compared to the intervention.

You can normally deal with confounding variables using some form of random allocation to conditions. We will discuss the options you have in detail in later chapters.

By contrast, an **extraneous variable** is often easier to deal with. Excluding the independent variable, these are any variables that could affect your dependent variable, but not in a way that aligns to your independent variable. Extraneous variables often include:

* Environmental factors such as time of day.
* Ambient temperature and noise levels.
* Expected variations in classroom activity and delivery.

For example, if you wanted to measure maths performance with a maths test (following two different teaching methods), it is plausible a noisy room or a broken boiler could affect performance on the test. These variables may not make everyone worse (or everyone better) but they will act to introduce extra variation into your data, so the best thing to do is to try to keep these extraneous variables constant. You cannot remove extraneous variables altogether, unlike confounding variables. Nonetheless, you can minimise their impact. This is often quite simple to do – for example by always running your experiment at the same time of day or keeping the classroom lighting consistent and the room at a comfortable temperature.

Writing your hypothesis

Once you have identified your research aim and the independent and dependent variables, you are in a position to create a hypothesis. As we discussed in Chapter 1, this needs to be a testable statement. Technically speaking, when designing an experimental research study you should write two different types of hypothesis.

Types of hypothesis

The first of the two types of hypothesis you need to know about is the **null hypothesis**. The null hypothesis predicts that your independent variable will have no effect on your dependent variable. The second type is an **experimental hypothesis** (sometimes called a research hypothesis). In contrast, the experimental hypothesis predicts that the independent variable will have an effect on the dependent variable.

In reality, you rarely see the null hypothesis stated formally in research plans or reports but, for the sake of completeness, we have included it here. Let's put both of these in the context of a simple example. Imagine you have a research aim to find out whether mindfulness training affects children's well-being. Your independent variable could be operationally defined as follows:

> IV level 1 (control condition) – No mindfulness training
>
> IV level 2 (experimental condition) – Mindfulness training

Your dependent variable could be a simple scale called the 'well-being scale', completed by the children. From this information the following hypotheses can be developed:

> Null hypothesis – Mindfulness training will have *no* effect on children's well-being scale scores.
>
> Experimental hypothesis – Mindfulness training will have *an* effect on children's well-being scale scores.

As you read the experimental hypothesis above, you might have been thinking that it was a bit vague, because it only suggested an effect and not the direction of the effect (i.e. whether well-being is improved or worsened by the mindfulness training). In fact, it is possible to be more specific in your experimental hypotheses, as you will now learn.

The direction of your hypothesis

The example hypothesis we gave you above did not state the direction of any effect. This means, in theory, that the statement would be supported if the mindfulness training altered well-being scores in either of two different directions – either increasing or decreasing well-being. This kind of hypothesis is referred to as a **bidirectional** or **two-tailed hypothesis** (the reasoning for this will become clear later).

The alternative to a bidirectional hypothesis is one that does specify which direction the effect will be in. This type of hypothesis is called a **directional** or **one-tailed hypothesis**. If we had assumed that mindfulness would improve well-being (and thus increase scores on the scale), our directional experimental hypothesis would look like this:

> Mindfulness will have a *positive* effect on children's well-being, increasing well-being scale scores.

In most cases, particularly when you are interested in things like attainment, you are most likely to be setting a one-tailed hypothesis, as you are unlikely to want to put in place an intervention that you think is possibly going to do harm. This said, if your study is comparing two things and you are unsure whether they are better or worse than each other then you will have a two-tailed hypothesis.

The difference between the two types of hypothesis may appear to be small, but ultimately it makes a big difference to the statistics you will end up reporting (as you will learn later on). For this reason, it is important that you have decided whether your hypothesis will be one-tailed or two-tailed before you start.

Learning Zone 2.3. Constructing your hypothesis

Now that you have learned how to write a hypothesis, make a note of the null and experimental hypotheses for the research aim you selected independent and dependent variables for earlier.

Once you have drafted them, think about whether they are one-tailed or two-tailed and be sure this is what you want.

Brain Box 2.4. Perfecting your hypothesis phrasing

There are different views about whether to state a hypothesis in the present tense or the future tense (i.e. by using the word 'will' within the sentence). In many cases, this comes down to individual preference. However, some people argue that if you use the future tense then you are actually making a prediction. Writing in the present tense, the way we will describe the hypothesis in this book from now on, has an advantage. Ultimately, it can more easily become the title of your paper, journal article or conference style poster presentation. For example:

Lessons involving sustained outdoor fieldwork improve geography GCSE attainment in an urban secondary school.

It is also a matter of preference as to how operational to make your hypothesis (i.e. the level of detail you include in it). However, as a general principle, including some detail is probably a good idea when you are designing your research, because it can help to focus your mind on the rest of the research design and areas such as the procedures and materials you are using. For example, using a hypothesis about group work and maths there could be a number of levels of operational definition:

> Null hypothesis – Two lessons of group work does not improve column addition problem-solving.

> Experimental hypothesis – Two lessons of group work improves column addition problem-solving.

Or with a little more detail:

> Null hypothesis – Two lessons of group work does not improve column addition problem-solving in a rural English primary school.

> Experimental hypothesis – Two lessons of group work improves column addition problem-solving in a rural English primary school.

Or with even more detail:

> Null hypothesis – Two lessons of group work does not improve column addition problem-solving in a rural English primary school, as measured by number of items in a 30-item 10-minute test.

> Experimental hypothesis – Two lessons of group work improves column addition problem-solving in a rural English primary school, as measured by number of items in a 30-item 10-minute test.

Test yourself 2

Question 1

A researcher hypothesises that reducing lesson time will have an effect on attainment in English. Is this a one-tailed or two-tailed hypothesis?

Question 2

You are interested in testing whether pupils learn better in groups of one gender or both genders. Suggest some levels of the independent variable (gender balance) that you could use.

Question 3

Explain what 'reliability of a dependent variable' means.

What next?

Now that you have learned how to draft scientific hypotheses, the next stage is to understand how to conduct the experiment to test them. In the next chapter we will look at how you design an experiment – that is, working out what you will do with the participants and what you will measure. We will begin with simple designs and build to more complex designs.

Chapter 3

Designing experimental research

By the end of this chapter, you will know about:

- Various different ways to design experiments.
- The advantages and disadvantages of these designs.
- What is meant by the term 'randomised controlled trial'.
- How to include more than two conditions in your research.

Learning the subject that is experimental design

Whether you use qualitative or quantitative experimental research, the key is making sure you design your experiment appropriately. Different designs are suitable for addressing different research questions. Understanding this is essential because different research questions, contexts and participant groups are better addressed with different forms of research design. If you choose a design that is less able to investigate your particular research question, it will, in the end, weaken your ability to interpret your results and come to any clear conclusions.

Where this topic is also taught in schools

Experimental design is a subject that is taught in psychology at AS and A level as well as at university across a wide range of disciplines. It uses terminology that has specific meanings so it is important to use the terms accurately. You would not grade a colleague's GCSE or A level history lesson very highly if the teacher insisted that the First World War began in 1912, would you? The same subject knowledge expectations apply to this topic. Getting the experimental research terminology and the analysis of your data right is essential. This imperative is amplified by the fact that you, and the teachers you work with, may well want to go on to involve the pupils you use in the study when you debrief them or explain what you have done, or even teach them to use experimental research designs within your own subject. Some of these pupils may well be studying areas of the curriculum that cover knowledge related to what we are teaching you here, such as A level psychology.

Getting it right

The number one rule when it comes to experimental design is the maxim, if you put garbage in, you will get garbage out. In other words, if you do not do everything you can to choose the best-fit type of experimental design, and apply it with care and rigour to the question you are interested in, the results are not going to be worth very much at all.

Creating the right research design is not only challenging but it can also be highly rewarding – if only as an exercise in critical thinking. Indeed, several of the teachers we have worked with recently have begun to teach scientific method to their children as part of a range of subject areas.

Time commitments in quantitative and qualitative research

There will be differences in the time you end up allocating to the various aspects of your study when you do quantitative research compared to qualitative. It is important to consider this before embarking on your study. In some forms of qualitative research (such as focus group research or semi-structured interviews) you may not take that long to design your list of open interview questions and pilot them. However, once you have the data you will most likely end up spending a considerable amount of time transcribing the interviews, analysing the language and figuring out what your findings are.

Quantitative experimental research can often involve the opposite time allocation. It can take a long time to design your research and identify (or create) some appropriate numerical measures to use in your research. It can then take even more effort to randomise and organise your participants while maintaining the protocols around the treatments you are going to use. In contrast to qualitative research, once you have inputted the data, the results in quantitative experimental studies usually appear in an instant in your statistical computer package or in an online version of a test.

Writing up your research involves pretty much the same effort whether you do quantitative or qualitative research. In Chapter 7, we will look at a straightforward way to do this so you can present your results either in a conference poster format (the way postgraduates often present their findings at university conferences on the journey to writing up their research in journal articles and in their final thesis) or in the format of a journal article.

Your starter for ten

Once you have settled on your hypothesis (see Chapter 2), it is necessary to think very carefully about how you will test it. This is rarely a straightforward decision and there are often a number of options with regard to how you could run the experiment.

Let's take the example we used previously about mindfulness. Our one-tailed experimental hypothesis was:

> Mindfulness training will have a positive effect on children's well-being scale scores.

Spend a minute or two thinking about how you could construct an experiment to test this hypothesis.

From this hypothesis, two options for testing it come to mind relatively easily. The first approach would be to have two groups of children and give one group mindfulness training (experimental condition) and the second group no training (control condition), and then measure their well-being using the scale. A second approach would be to have all the children take part in both conditions and measure their well-being after each one. These two possibilities are called a between-participant and within-participant design, respectively. We will go into these two designs in more detail below.

These are not the only designs you could use, but they are a great place to start your thinking when you are planning a piece of experimental research. Like all areas of research, the design you use will depend on your research aims, the population you have drawn your sample from and practicalities related to what you can do in the context in which you are implementing your study. The last of these (context) is particularly important and often overlooked. Making your experiment workable, so that it easily fits within the context you are dealing with, is important both practically and (as you will learn later) in terms of interpreting your results.

Between-participant post-test design

Stepping out of education for a moment so we can use a straightforward example, imagine if our research aim was to find out whether alcohol consumption inhibits driving performance. Our independent variable would be the amount of alcohol consumed, perhaps with the levels of the independent variable defined as follows:

> IV level 1 (control condition) – No alcohol consumption before driving
>
> IV level 2 (intervention) – Double the legal alcohol limit before driving

The dependent variable could be the number of cones left standing *after* driving around an obstacle course (we hasten to add that our imaginary obstacle course is in a safe off-road location!). From our design we can devise a hypothesis – we have opted for a one-tailed hypothesis because we think we can predict the direction of the result:

> Alcohol will have a negative effect on driving skills as measured by performance around an obstacle course.

The simplest form of experiment would be to have our population divided into two groups, with half being in the control condition and half in the experimental condition. This is called a between-participant design because we are comparing the differences *between* two different groups of people. You may also find it referred to as an independent measures, between-groups, between-subject or, more rarely, an independent samples design.

More specifically, we would call this particular design a **between-participant post-test design** because we are only measuring the effect of our intervention after it has taken place. This type of design is illustrated in Figure 3.1.

This type of design is appealing because it is simple to conduct. There are, however, limitations to it and these need to be carefully considered. Take a moment to pull apart the design above, note what flaws you notice and what issues the design throws up. You may want to jot down your ideas. The types of problems you are most likely to have thought of first are things like:

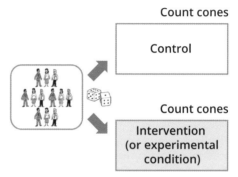

- The people in the two groups are different so they may have different driving abilities and experience.

- The people in the two groups may have different levels of tolerance to alcohol consumption.

Figure 3.1. A between-participant post-test design with a measure of the dependent variable collected after the intervention.

These two issues relate to the main disadvantage of using a between-participant post-test design. Namely, that you have two different groups of people and therefore any differences between the groups caused by your independent variable could be confounded by variations in the background or abilities of the participants who make up the two groups (i.e. their individual differences).

One way to deal with these individual differences is to use **random allocation** to put people into the different groups – this is the process of **randomisation**. To illustrate why this is important let's take a classroom-based example.

Imagine you taught maths and you decided on a between-participant design to test the effectiveness of a new approach. On the day of the experiment you wait for pupils to arrive at the door. If you allocated the first 15 children to arrive in the classroom to one condition and the remaining 15 to another condition, you might find that you have all the enthusiastic ones in the first condition because they turned up promptly. This could make enthusiasm a confounding variable. By contrast, if you randomly allocated each individual to a condition then you would spread out the enthusiastic pupils between your two conditions.

You can randomise in a variety of simple ways, including rolling a die for the condition each person should go in (even number = experimental condition, odd number = control condition) or you can use more sophisticated approaches in Excel. Of course, randomisation is a chance process and there is always a risk that you will end up with an imbalance anyway. Therefore, in Chapter 4, we will show you some more sophisticated forms of randomisation that can mitigate this risk.

Brain Box 3.1. Randomisation, random allocation and random sampling

A common error people make all the time is to use the terms 'random sampling' and 'random allocation' as if they are the same thing. They are not. You should use the term random allocation when you randomly *allocate* your participants to the condition they will experience (or the order that they will experience the conditions in your study). **Random sampling** (sometimes called random selection) is completely different and involves randomly selecting people from a population you have access to in order to then use them in your study. There is more to this than hair-splitting because the two strategies do very different things to improve the strength of the claims that you can make about the research findings in your final report.

The benefits of random allocation compared to random sampling

Random allocation improves the internal validity of your study by removing experimenter bias with regard to the decision about who does what (there is more on this in Chapter 4). This means that random allocation improves the extent to which your study can be classed as a true experiment. On the other hand, random sampling also removes bias but only with regard to the choice of people that you involve in your study. Random sampling can thus enhance the claim that your participants represent an unbiased example of a group drawn from the population you are interested in studying.

Where random allocation improves the internal reliability of a study, random sampling improves a study's external validity (or ecological validity) by being able to 'infer' that your results also apply to the wider population from which your sample was drawn. Clearly, a study that has used random sampling and random allocation has pushed both buttons and can perhaps (depending on the quality of other aspects of the design and the correct statistical analysis) make a greater claim than a study that has just randomly allocated.

Other ways to reduce individual differences in a between-participant design

As well as randomisation, you could also reduce the impact of individual differences by using a very large sample (number of participants). The theory behind this type of approach is that as your sample size increases, the two groups being tested will get more and more similar. Unfortunately, although an ostensibly good solution (generally it is better to have more participants), you will probably need to do more than this.

A better solution than just going to a massive sample size, and a typical way of tackling the problem, might be to draw your sample from a very similar group of people. For example, you might use only males who are between the ages of 18 and 23 and who completed their driving test within the last month. Another partial solution would be to have a pre-test (i.e. the participants would all drive around the course of cones before then completing the two conditions). This would then give you a baseline assessment of the drivers' existing abilities and the option to check that they all started from a similar level of ability.

However, a pre-test may not always be possible. Suppose the thing you were testing did not exist until you began the intervention – for example, if you were testing the impact of an intervention on completely brand new knowledge that you are certain the children did not know before the experiment began.

Between-participant pre- and post-test design

You may already be familiar with the **between-participant pre- and post-test design** because this kind of experimental design is quite common in education research. It follows the same principle as the previous design in that you expose two randomly allocated groups to different conditions.

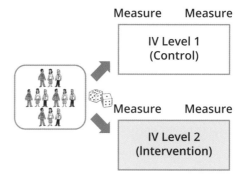

Figure 3.2. A two-condition between-participant pre- and post-test design.

It is slightly different to the post-test only model in that there is a pre-test of the dependent variable before the treatment begins.

Having a pre-test allows you to a check for similar performance prior to manipulation of the independent variable. This kind of design is illustrated in Figure 3.2.

Another solution to the issue of individual differences is to consider a different design, whereby participants take part in both conditions. This type of design is a within-participant design (also referred to as within-subject, repeated measures or cross-over design).

Within-participant design

In a **within-participant design**, the participants complete all the conditions. In the case of our example study into the effect of alcohol consumption on driving performance, half of the participants would begin the process by driving around the cones sober, then on another (second) occasion they would drive around the same set of cones, this time following the consumption of alcohol. The other half of the participants would begin the research by driving around the cones drunk and then, following a period of time long enough for the effects to have worn off, they would drive around for the second time when sober (see Figure 3.3).

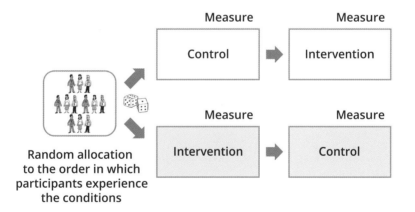

Figure 3.3. A counterbalanced within-participant design with two conditions.

Counterbalancing a within-participant design

The deliberate reversal of the order in which one group does the two conditions is called **counterbalancing**. This is necessary because the experience of doing something once may change subsequent responses. This is because people have the somewhat annoying tendency to learn things, often in response to experiencing them just once! Because of this participants tend to be better at a task the second time around, irrespective of your manipulation of the independent variable. In the driving example, a second experience of the obstacle course could improve performance in itself. The opposite can also occur as people get bored or fatigued by a particular activity, so when they encounter the experience again they might pay less attention and perhaps perform worse. We call these **order effects** (sometimes referred to as fatigue effects or practice effects).

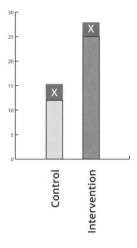

Counterbalancing reduces the impact of order effects because, if half the participants do the conditions in the reverse order, no one condition has benefitted more from the order in which they were presented. In Figure 3.4 you can see the theory in practice. Here we have amalgamated the scores for two groups of people who have both completed a counterbalanced control condition and an intervention. The area at the top of each bar shows a theoretical inflation of scores that may have taken place in response to the second time participants conducted the test. However, because the order effect exists in both halves of the data, the effects cancel themselves out.

Figure 3.4. How counterbalancing can theoretically offset carry-over effects by cancelling them out.

As well as counterbalancing in a within-participant design, it is still necessary to use randomisation but, rather than randomly allocating participants to a single condition, you randomly allocate them to the order in which they experience the two conditions.

Other benefits of a within-participant design

In a within-participant design the participants are effectively acting as their own control. This means that, in most cases, you do not necessarily need to apply a pre-test. This said, there might be times when you want a pre-test – for example, when your hypothesis is to do with progress rather than attainment, and you need a pre-test so you can see how much gain the participants made during the treatment period.

As well as reducing the impact of individual differences, there is another more practical advantage to within-participant designs. If you had 60 participants in total and you used a between-participant design, 30 would do the control and 30 would do the intervention. However, with a within-participant design, because your 60 participants would end up doing both the control condition and the intervention, you would end up with twice the amount of data with which to compare the effects of your intervention with the control. This would make your design equivalent to a between-participant design with 120 participants.

Having a wash-out period in a within-participant design

As you read about the impact of alcohol consumption example above, you may have been wondering how the participants can complete the condition of sobriety after alcohol consumption. Obviously, alcohol stays in the body for a period of time, so for that reason it would be necessary to introduce a 'wash-out period' between the two conditions. For alcohol consumption, the wash-out period might only need to be 24–48 hours; for other things you might experiment on, more or less than that. A wash-out period helps to avoid **carry-over effects** (i.e. the effects of one condition carrying over to the second condition). The idea of a wash-out period is illustrated in Figure 3.5.

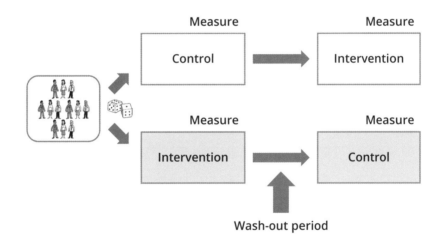

Figure 3.5. A counterbalanced within-participant design with a wash-out period.

A wash-out period could be necessary in a classroom study to avoid the effects of one pedagogy carrying over into the next condition.

When you can't use a within-participant design

Having read all this you may be thinking, why would anyone bother with a between-participant design at all? The answer to that question is really quite simple. You can't use a within-participant design when the effects of your treatment are irreversible. For example (and we are not suggesting you try this at home!), if you wanted to explore whether chopping off someone's leg inhibited their running performance, you could certainly randomly allocate one group to becoming leg-less while the other group keep their legs, and they both run the same course. However, if you attempted to use this in a within-participant design (you may want to look back at Figure 3.3 for a moment), although you could leave one group's leg on to run the control condition and then after that remove a leg so they can attempt to run the intervention condition, it will not work the other way round. Once the leg is removed, it is irreversible! You can't use a within-participant design when the effects of your treatment are irreversible.

The same principle would apply if you were looking at conducting a piece of education research in which the aim was to improve a particular area of knowledge or content (e.g. learning times tables by heart), where the research question is, as it were, 'content-bound'. Clearly, the children are not going to be able to unlearn the content that they have now learned. In this case, we have to use a between-participant design and find a way of managing the between-participant variation as best we can.

However, many of the teachers we have been working with (about 30–40%) have found excellent and appropriate ways to apply a within-participant design where their research is into a classroom process or form of pedagogy, rather than in the acquisition of specific content – in other words, the research design is process-orientated rather than content-bound.

Here is an example of the type of research design that is possible. The teacher's research aim is:

> To find out whether group work improves attainment in poetry writing compared to the usual approach of whole class teaching.

To avoid the issues described above, the teacher has designed two double length lessons (see Figure 3.6). One of these is focused on writing a poem about cities and the other a poem about the countryside. Both lessons will contain the same expectations with regard to applying the learning that the children have had about poetic devices, and they will be expected to produce similar length poems that will be marked at the end of each of the double length lessons (using the same mark scheme). Although the two double lessons will be delivered in the same order – 'cities' followed by 'the countryside' – a two-condition counterbalanced within-subject design will be embedded within these lessons (see Figure 3.6). In this design, the control condition will be the usual whole class pedagogy and the intervention will be the use of group work, with the two conditions counterbalanced.

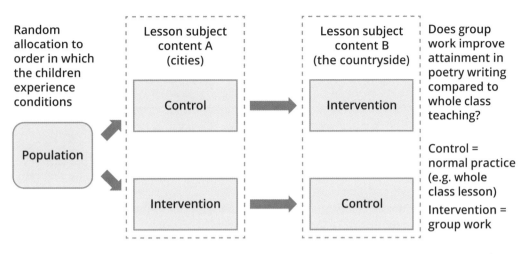

Figure 3.6. Example of a classroom-based within-participant design.

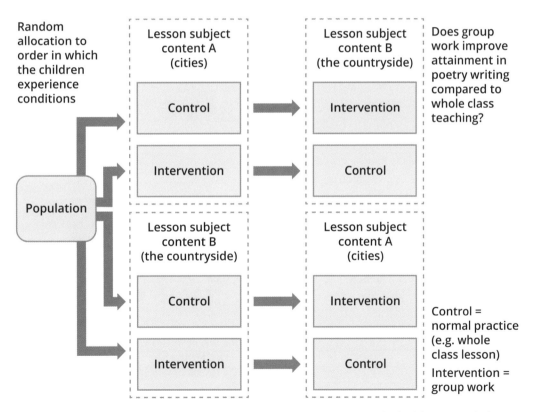

Figure 3.7. Example of a classroom-based within-participant design with 'double' counterbalancing.

A further refinement to control for order effect (related to having done the cities lesson before the countryside lesson) would be to double up the number of children involved and double counterbalance out these effects (as in Figure 3.7).

Matched pairs design

Earlier on, when we talked about the limitations of a between-participant design, we highlighted the obvious difficulty presented by using different participants in each condition. Namely, that you can end up measuring not the intervention that you exposed people to but the differences between them. We also pointed out that you can't use a within-participant design if the effects of your treatment are irreversible.

There is, however, another option that is an extension of the between-participant design. This is called a **matched pairs** (or case-matched) design. This type of design aims to produce similar benefits to the within-participant design with regard to reducing the individual differences between people in the study. To conduct a matched pairs design you begin by 'matching' up participants in pairs according to individual characteristics that you think might confound your research if you did not control for them. For example, the two highest attaining girls might be paired and the two highest attaining boys and so on. Once you have all your participants paired in such a way, you then randomly allocate each member of a pair to the control or intervention group. In this way, you force a balance of characteristics between your participant groups while also including randomisation. In Chapter 4 we will teach you how to do this in practice. Figure 3.8 gives an example of this type of approach.

Matched pairs designs have another advantage over between-participant designs – if you have a case-matched study you can use the same statistical approach that you are allowed to use in a within-participant design when it comes to the analysis. This is not a trivial point. The statistical tests that are suitable for a between-participant design are less forgiving than the ones you can use for a within-participant design, and therefore it is easier to identify significant results. Chapter 5 will explain this in detail and tell you which tests to use when.

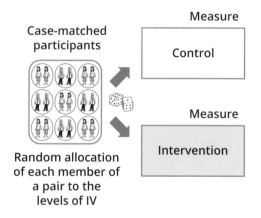

Figure 3.8. A two-condition matched pairs design.

Advantages and disadvantages of different designs

Between-participant design

The advantages of a using a between-participant design can be summarised as follows:

- Participants in a between-participant design only need to complete one condition, so providing that the other conditions are implemented at the same time, it is possible to obtain results for the study more quickly than with a within-participant design.

- Participants can be randomly allocated to different conditions, thereby creating a separation between the two conditions and avoiding 'cross-contamination'.

- There are no carry-over or order effects as the participants have been exposed only once to the experimental condition (in contrast to a within-participant design where participants are exposed to all the conditions one after another).

- Participants are less likely to become bored or suffer from fatigue as they complete multiple versions of the same questionnaire or test.

The disadvantages of a using a between-participant design can be summarised as follows:

- You need a lot more participants in order to detect an effect. This is because between-participant designs need analysis with more stringent statistical tests. In addition, whereas in a within-participant design each participant produces multiple amounts of data, in a between-participant design this is not the case. This means it can take longer to recruit the participant numbers needed.

- It may be harder to control for some extraneous variables (e.g. time of day, teacher) that could potentially become confounding variables.

- There may still be differences between participants that have not been dealt with during the randomisation process. These differences may, if great enough, affect both the internal validity and reliability of your results.

Within-participant design

The advantages of a using a within-participant design can be summarised as follows:

- You need far fewer participants within your study as you reuse the same participants for each condition. This can reduce the overall time that it takes to conduct a study because you do not waste as much time recruiting. In parallel, the statistics that you use for the analysis of this type of design are far more forgiving that the ones you must use for a between-participant design.

- The risk that individual differences between participants may confound your results is greatly reduced because each participant is effectively acting as their own control.

- As each participant is acting as their own control, depending on your research question, this can allow for a simpler design and for it not being necessary to have a pre-test within the design.

The disadvantages of a using a within-participant design can be summarised as follows:

- You can't use a within-participant design where the effects of any of the interventions (or conditions) are irreversible.

- People can improve their performance (or may change it) just because they have done an element of the research before, particularly a test. Even if you deal with this with a sufficient wash-out period, counterbalancing and testing to see if these effects may be present, you will still need to acknowledge this as a potential limitation.

- Participant fatigue can be an issue if participants become affected by completing the same tests over and over again.

- Because participants may begin to guess the purpose of the study, there may be an amplification of demand characteristics (i.e. the tendency of participants to please the experimenter by doing what they think the task demands). In contrast, in a between-participant (or matched pairs) design, it is possible to keep participants blind to the other condition(s).

Matched pairs design

As we discussed above, matched pairs design is a variant of the between-participant design. It therefore has the advantages of a between-participant design and in addition:

- Case-matching your participants as tightly with each other as possible can help you to control for individual differences, in some cases as well as if you had a within-participant design.
- Where there is a risk of carry-over (or order effects), it is a better choice than a within-participant design.

However, there are also disadvantages to a matched pairs design:

- It can be very time consuming to match participants.
- The effectiveness of the design is only as good as the quality of your matching and it is impossible to do this perfectly.
- It can sometimes be difficult to find enough participants who are similar enough to be case-matched, thus reducing the potential sample size.

What is a randomised controlled trial exactly?

So far in this chapter we have talked about three different types of experimental design, from quite simple designs to more complex designs (between-participant, within-participant and matched pairs). You will notice that we have not introduced you to a specific design for a **randomised controlled trial (RCT)**. The reason for this is that you could use any one of the designs above in this kind of trial, provided it fulfils the following criteria:

- It uses randomisation to reduce experimenter bias when manipulating the independent variable.
- It incorporates a control condition.

Figure 3.9 shows how the terminology might apply to a between-participant design.

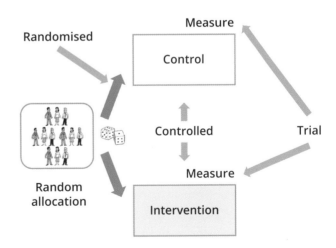

Figure 3.9. The term randomised controlled trial when applied to a between-participant design.

Types of control condition in a randomised controlled trial

In a randomised controlled trial, a control condition could be no intervention at all (i.e. doing nothing and therefore no effects are expected) – this is called a **negative control**. Alternatively, it can be a current existing practice against which a new intervention is being compared (i.e. some effect is expected) – this is called a **positive control**. In some cases, a study may have both types of control.

In education research, it is this latter form (the positive control) which is almost always going to be the case. Clearly, it would not only be unethical to deny a group of children schooling completely compared to another group but it would also be pretty futile, as any good teaching in relation to a new topic is obviously going to be better than no teaching of the topic.

Practically, from a teacher-led research perspective, this means that you are ideally going to plan the control condition lessons as carefully as the intervention ones so that your control lessons reflect normal practice. Of course, there could be exceptions where a negative control could be both useful and ethical. An example might occur where there is uncertainty about the effect of attending an expensive summer school or not, and a trial is then undertaken to see if the money would be better spent helping the children in other ways.

Non-randomised controlled trials

There are also times when you simply cannot randomise and need a quasi-experimental design because you have naturally occurring levels to your independent variable (as discussed in Chapter 2) – for example, when you are interested in comparing the relative performance of boys and girls to a single treatment. Alternatively, it may be that randomisation is impossible for practical reasons.

Richard is a participant in a non-randomised clinical trial at this very moment. To cut a long story short, after going to Saudi Arabia with the visa he got (after being stressed in the post office), he managed to contract meningococcal meningitis. Fortunately, he didn't lose any fingers or we might still be writing. Anyway, while in hospital he was asked if he would participate in a trial. This trial is looking into the effect of the form of meningitis that he had on his genetic make-up. Somewhere, there is someone else that he is being directly compared to, and this will have been done using a stringent form of case-matching so that the person he is being compared to is, to all intents and purposes, the same (oh my!). There was no way that the researchers could have known that Richard was going to turn up and no 'treatment' that they could randomly allocate him to, so he is now part of a non-randomised matched pairs study into genetic change in response to exposure to meningitis.

If you didn't case-match, but compared similar groups in similar schools, you might say you were doing a 'non-randomised parallel group design', as was the case with the recent study that appeared in the *British Journal of Psychiatry* into the positive effects of mindfulness in schools.[1] In this study, the authors decided to title it a 'non-randomised controlled feasibility study' because you can't really claim causality if you have not randomly allocated – a point we will return to in the next chapter.

Including a third condition in your design

There may be times when having just two conditions (e.g. control and intervention) in your study is not enough. This may be because you need to control for something other than existing classroom practice (your positive control condition). In such situations it is common to add a third condition.

Supposing your mathematics intervention consisted of pupils being withdrawn from class to complete a specific scheme of work for 20 minutes each week. You may want to find out whether it was the actual maths pedagogy being used in the session that made a difference or whether it was just getting 20 minutes of one-to-one support. Therefore, you might operationally define your independent variable as follows:

IV level 1 – Normal classroom practice

IV level 2 – Withdraw with general maths help

IV level 3 – Withdraw and follow the specific scheme of work

It is also acceptable and efficient to trial two different interventions at the same time.

IV level 1 (control condition) – Normal classroom practice

IV level 2 (experimental condition) – Intervention A

IV level 3 (experimental condition) – Intervention B

You might do this to test two types of spelling strategy at once against normal practice. Just as with two-condition designs, three-condition designs can be between-participant or within-participant as illustrated in Figure 3.10 and 3.11.

You could also have a three-condition case-matched design, if you match trios rather than pairs prior to randomisation.

---

1   W. Kuyken, K. Weare, O. C. Ukoumunne, R. Vicary, N. Motton, R. Burnett, C. Cullen, S. Hennelly and F. Huppert, 'Effectiveness of the Mindfulness in Schools Programme: non-randomised controlled feasibility study', *British Journal of Psychiatry* 203(2) (2013): 126–131.

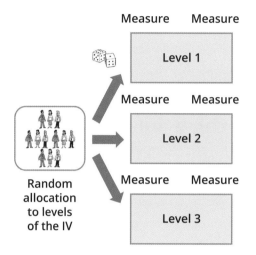

Figure 3.10. Between-participant pre- and post-test design with three conditions.

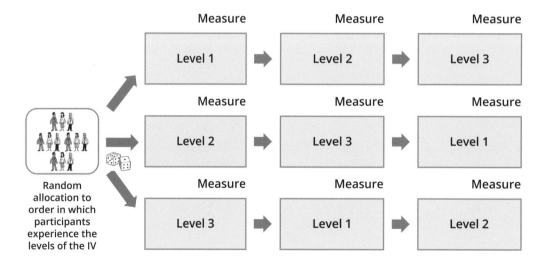

Figure 3.11. A counterbalanced post-test only within-participant design with three conditions.

Brain Box 3.2. An example of a teacher-led within-participant design with three levels to the independent variable

Charlotte Morris conducted a within-participant design with three levels to the independent variable and counterbalancing. She tested the efficacy of three different spelling strategies. The levels of her independent variable were as follows:

IV level 1 (control condition) – Normal teacher practice without video delivery

IV level 2 (intervention A) – Teacher on video delivering general (active) spelling strategy

IV level 3 (intervention B) – Using the look, cover, check, write (LCCW) approach delivered by the same teacher on video

Charlotte's research also illustrates an innovative way of controlling for teacher variation in the delivery of the different conditions. She videoed the instructional component of each of the lessons so that she could appear talking directly to the children in all of the various schools that the research took place in – with a teacher from those schools facilitating to support the delivery. In total, 88 pupils took part in the study.[2]

Test yourself 3

Question 1

What are individual differences, and why do they cause problems in between-participant but not within-participant designs?

Question 2

A researcher interested in PE preparation has a small team of pupils and wants to evaluate the effects of a modified set of warm-up activities on a stamina test. What kind of design would be most suitable, and what could the different conditions be?

Question 3

Why is it necessary to counterbalance conditions?

2   Charlotte Morris' study is also written up in Churches and McAleavy, *Evidence That Counts*.

What next?

In the next chapter, we will discuss a wide range of considerations that are necessary when you actually implement your research. This will include the impact of the researchers' and the participants' expectations and how to use different types of randomisation.

Chapter 4

Implementing your study

By the end of this chapter, you will know about:

- The impact of the researcher and participant on the experiment.
- The different types of randomisation and how to use them.
- How to create a research plan.

Turning your design into successful research

Having appropriate dependent and independent variables in a suitable research design is not enough on its own to ensure that your research is successful. Applying scientific method is all about trying to develop an experiment that is as objective as possible.

The truth is, we (participants and researchers) all have biases, many of which are unconscious. Therefore, you need to find ways to deal with those biases and personal presuppositions within your experiment, if you are going to obtain a result that represents what is really going on rather than what these biases might lead you to hope or assume is happening. If you don't do this you will make errors.

These errors become more and more important if they could lead you to make claims for your research that are not accurate. This is particularly important if you undertake research that could have serious implications for others. Of course, replication of a study helps, but it is also important to make sure that you do things in the best way possible right from the start. In order for you to understand this topic, we are going to begin by dealing with participant and researcher effects before looking in detail at randomisation.

Participant effects

As well as considering the effects of variables, both desired and not desired (i.e. confounding and extraneous variables), it is important to consider the impact of the people involved in the research, including the participants. When participants take part in an experiment they will form an impression of what the study is about and may change their behaviour to fit that impression. This impression can be formed from what they may have heard about the study, the setting of the study or something the researcher says or does. Irrespective of the basis of these feelings, they result in **demand characteristics** (i.e. participants doing what they think the task demands). You can think of these demand characteristics as a type of extraneous variable.

Dealing with and avoiding demand characteristics

Demand characteristics are more likely to arise in within-participant designs because the participant takes part in all conditions and therefore knows what happens in all of them, which means they form a fuller impression. However, demand characteristics can also affect between-participant designs if the participants can gain enough of a sense of the study from other sources.

There are a number of ways to reduce the effect of demand characteristics. One way this can be done is with written or videoed instructions. Another way is to deceive the participants about the nature of the study. There are obvious ethical implications that arise from deceiving participants; however, mild deception of participants in experimental research in an education setting is unlikely to cause harm. So, withholding full details of everything that is going on may be justified if it means your findings are valid in the end. There are many occasions in the classroom when you use a degree of minor deception already. For example, you would not open a lesson by talking about the pedagogical theory that underpins your lesson, nor would you talk to a primary school pupil in a one-to-one session about the extent to which you can see their emerging levels according to Piaget's theories.

Irrespective of the level of deception, you should take responsibility for debriefing the participants after the research is completed. This debrief should include the nature of the deception and an explanation of its purpose. In addition, you should give the participants the opportunity to express their feelings regarding the approach used. People can become upset if they find that they have been deceived and may even spot it themselves. Thus, a fundamental principle should be to apply deception only to a minimum and only if it is necessary to avoid confounding the research.

An alternative to deceiving the participants about the nature of the experiment in its entirety, and an approach commonly used in drugs trials, is to conduct a **blind experiment**. This means that the participant is not aware of what condition they are in. In a drugs trial, for example, the experimental group would get the test drug and those in the control group would get a treatment that looks (and maybe tastes and smells) the same as the test drug – this is sometimes called a placebo. In an educational setting, it may be harder to do this if your intervention consists of a new pedagogy dramatically different to anything your children have experienced before. However, it may still be possible, provided you design your control condition appropriately.

Learning Zone 4.1. Briefing your participants

Think about a research design that you are planning to implement and consider the following:

- What will you tell the participants?
- What will you tell other teachers?
- How will you manage the data, and what will you say about this?
- How will you debrief the participants afterwards?
- Is your head teacher able to give permission, or do you need to seek other consent?

Mundane realism

Another way to avoid participant effects is to build high levels of **mundane realism** into your research. Mundane realism is the extent to which the protocol that your participants experience, or even the entire research study, is similar to activities or processes that the participants would possibly experience in day-to-day life. Having high levels of mundane realism means that participants are less likely to form specific impressions, which enhances your ability to claim that the results represent what would happen in the real world. Mundane realism therefore improves external validity and your ability to claim that your findings are generalisable.

In a school context, the types of things that you could apply to enhance your study's mundane realism include:

- Building the study into and around an existing timetable process.
- Using the children's real teachers and resources.
- Being everyday and matter-of-fact with participants when briefing them, if you need to.
- Using the classrooms that the children experience their lessons in normally.
- Making the resources look like the type of resources that are usually used.
- If your study involves classroom observation of something that could be counted, consider using an unobtrusive process, such as a classroom equipped with video where the children are already accustomed to its use.
- If you do end up sitting in a classroom and observing, perhaps tie this in with the performance management cycle so the children are less likely to see it as something out of the ordinary.

Learning Zone 4.2. Building in mundane realism

Take one of your ideas for a research project and, for each of the areas below, think of ways that you could enhance the mundane realism of the conditions and protocols that the children will experience and the teachers will use.

- The materials that will be used by the children and teachers.
- The things that will be said to the children and teachers before you begin.
- The type of test you will use.
- The sort of things that the children will be asked to do.
- The time of day that the research will take place.
- The rooms where the research will take place.

Experimenter effects

Experimenter effects are closely related to participant effects. The term **experimenter effect** is used to describe any subtle signals or unconscious biases of the researcher that may affect the participants' responses and therefore the outcome of the study. These biases could arise from the way in which the participants are allocated to a condition or verbal and non-verbal cues given as they guide the participant through the process.

The process of randomisation can mitigate against the biases impacting on what condition a participant is in (or the order of conditions). But what about the cues a researcher might give to participants in the different conditions? Again, one approach is to use standardised written instructions to avoid the different conditions receiving different cues; however, this could be tricky when you are testing some classroom interventions. Another solution is to employ a **double-blind experiment**. In a blind experiment the participant is not aware of the condition that they are in; in a double-blind experiment neither is the researcher. This is not always possible because it does require someone to assist you with the randomisation, and in a classroom-based study you may well know what group the children are in because you are teaching them. However, where possible you can measure the dependent variables blind to the condition. For example, if the dependent variable was maths performance, you can mark all the maths tests without knowledge of which child they belong to until the marking is complete or until the end of the data collection phase. You could also find a colleague to mark your tests who doesn't know what you have been researching or who was in the control or intervention group.

Randomisation

As we have already discussed, randomisation is often used to allocate participants to different conditions (in a between-participant design) or to the order in which participants complete the conditions (in a within-participant design). The reason this is done, wherever possible, is because randomisation is a key way to deal with experimenter effects and biases (see Brain Box 4.1).

Brain Box 4.1. The difference between using randomisation and trying to be unbiased

The three examples below illustrate how three studies can look very similar on the surface but, in fact, result in very different levels of internal validity and thus very different levels of claim that the researcher can make with regard to the findings.

The design in Figure 4.1 lacks any form of randomisation. No matter how much the researcher claims that they were unbiased in their selection of participants, they have laid themselves open to the charge that they may have been biased in some way, even if that bias was unconscious. Non-randomised experiments do take place sometimes in situations where it is impossible to randomise (as described in Chapter 3). However, because

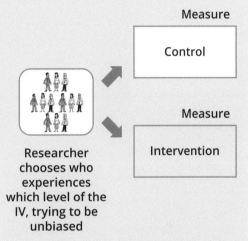

Figure 4.1. Design with researcher choice about who is in the control and intervention.

they cannot claim to have really established a causal relationship in the way that a randomised experiment can, it is normal to say that they provide 'preliminary evidence' or to title them as a 'feasibility study'. In other words, they have established the efficacy of the research design but have not really established the effect of the treatment.

Figure 4.2, on the other hand, has made use of random allocation. The form of randomisation is simple, however, and there is always the possibility that chance has produced very different participant groups.

Figure 4.3 is a much stronger design than those described in Figures 4.1 and 4.2. Not only has random allocation to control and intervention removed experimenter bias in terms of who went where, but the internal validity of the design has been enhanced further by pairing up the participants on critical case features (using case-matching) prior to randomisation. This has ensured that the randomisation has controlled for between-participant variation in terms of gender, prior attainment, ethnicity and special educational needs. We will explain how to do this in Excel shortly.

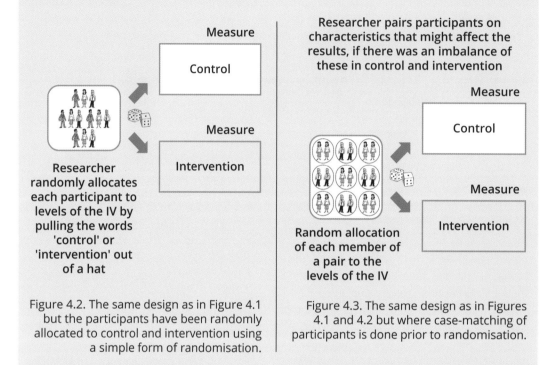

Figure 4.2. The same design as in Figure 4.1 but the participants have been randomly allocated to control and intervention using a simple form of randomisation.

Figure 4.3. The same design as in Figures 4.1 and 4.2 but where case-matching of participants is done prior to randomisation.

As well as helping to deal with bias, randomisation may also help to control for things like regression to the mean (the tendency of extreme scores (both high and low) on a pre-test to move in towards the average on a post-test) together with other unwelcome statistical effects.

On page 58 we will introduce another type of randomisation (stratified randomisation) which sits between simple randomisation and matched pairs randomisation with regard to the improvement of internal validity.

Types of randomisation

In this section, we are going to explore the advantages and disadvantages of several of the commonest ways to randomise. We are then going to take you systematically through the process of randomising using Excel with the first two of these. Once you know how to generate random numbers in Excel, and manipulate the columns around these numbers, you will be able to apply this to a range of contexts and situations.

The first two types of randomisation we are going to cover are simple randomisation and stratified randomisation. Later we will look at two other categories, pairwise randomisation and matched (or paired) randomisation.

Simple randomisation

Simple randomisation has the advantage of being easy to do and can be achieved simply by tossing a coin, picking names out of a hat or using tables of random numbers (which can often be found in the back of books on statistics). However, in this case, with simplicity also comes disadvantage. The disadvantage here is that simple randomisation processes can suffer from what is known as **chance bias**.

Chance bias occurs when randomisation, rather than resulting in two similar groups, in fact produces a considerable imbalance with regard to participant characteristics. For example, using a simple randomisation approach it is perfectly possible to end up with one group having the majority of the female pupils in it and none of the pupils with special educational needs. Such disadvantages can be partly mitigated by having a very large sample. But the truth is that all you are doing by going very large with your sample is reducing the probability that a really crazy chance bias will occur.

We will deal with some better ways to randomise later, but we will begin (in Brain Box 4.2) by teaching you how to do a simple randomisation in Excel, as it forms the basis for more sophisticated methods.

Brain Box 4.2. Simple randomisation in Excel

Before we start, if you don't know how to use Excel we suggest you stop for a minute and go online and find out how to do the following things: 'Copy', 'Paste' and 'Paste Special (Values)'. You will also need to know where to find the 'Functions' and the 'Sort' tools within the area known as 'Data'.

Step 1

Insert in a column the names of your participants. We will use column A for ease of discussion.

Step 2

Then click on the cell next to the first name in the column, which will be cell B1. Once you have done that type the following formula, exactly as it is below, leaving no spaces:

=RAND()

(If you know where to find 'Functions', you can also find this in the list of available functions.) Then press enter and Excel should produce a random number in the cell where previously the formula appeared. You then do this all the way down your list of names.

Step 3

Now you should have two columns – one with the participants' names in it and one with a random number (see Figure 4.4). There is one small problem with doing this in Excel, and this is that the numbers will re-randomise every time you do anything, so you need to fix the numbers so they don't change. Simply highlight the numbers column (B) and then copy and paste it back over itself – this time using the 'Paste Special' function and selecting 'Values' before you paste.

	A	B	C	D
1	Elza Ketner	0.167766		
2	Myles Paulding	0.036954		
3	Shelia Cooke	0.60812		
4	Daron Dane	0.428065		
5	Cleopatra Edington	0.242616		
6	Susanne Scogin	0.319268		
7	Merlyn Diederich	0.251479		
8	Phung Jansky	0.998963		

Figure 4.4. Allocation of random numbers to a list of names in Excel.

Step 4

The final step is to simply allocate the top half of the numbers to the control condition and the bottom half to the intervention and type in this information (see Figure 4.5). If you have an uneven number in your sample, you could toss a coin to send the last participant to control or intervention.

To do this, highlight your number column and click on 'Sort' and then 'Ascending'. You will be asked if you want to expand the selection, click OK. This will reorder the rows in ascending order of the random number. The top half goes to one condition and the bottom half to the other.

	A	B	C	D
1	Myles Paulding	0.036954	Control	
2	Elza Ketner	0.167766	Control	
3	Cleopatra Edington	0.242616	Control	
4	Merlyn Diederich	0.251479	Control	
5	Susanne Scogin	0.319268	Intervention	
6	Daron Dane	0.428065	Intervention	
7	Shelia Cooke	0.60812	Intervention	
8	Phung Jansky	0.998963	Intervention	

Figure 4.5. Participants sorted by lowest to highest random number and into control or intervention.

One short cut (if you are online while doing the above) is to go to one of the many sites that will generate a set of random numbers for you – for example, www.random.org enables you to generate a list of random numbers that you could then cut and paste into Excel before doing the split into control and intervention described above.

Stratified randomisation

As we have already discussed, when you use simple randomisation you can easily end up with unbalanced groups in terms of factors that we would prefer not to be unbalanced (such as gender or the percentage of pupils who are high ability or who have special educational needs). This problem can be solved if you make use of stratified randomisation.

In order to stratify and randomise at the same time you do the following. Start by defining the total number of possible blocks of 'participant type' that might occur. For example, if you wanted to ensure a balance of gender and special educational needs in control and intervention, you would need four blocks (see Figure 4.6): a block of pupils who are boys without special needs, a block of boys with special needs, a block of girls without special needs and a block of girls with special needs.

Once you have identified the pupils who fit within these blocks, do a simple randomisation on each block separately. When this is completed (and half of each block is in control or intervention) you can put them all back together using cut and paste.

Excel is rather helpful in this respect and can find the blocks very quickly (see Brain Box 4.3).

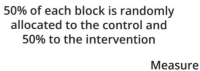

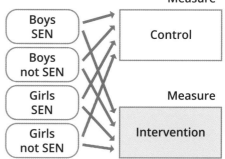

Figure 4.6. How stratified randomisation works.

Brain Box 4.3. How to do stratified randomisation in Excel

Begin as you normally would, putting the names of the participants in column A of a new Excel worksheet. Then in the columns to the right, add the information for each of the factors you want to control for in the experiment. In Figure 4.7, we have done this for special educational needs, gender and ethnicity.

Now you are going to use 'Sort' again, but this time highlight all four columns of data. Then right click and within the Sort menu choose 'Custom Sort'. This function will let you sort by a number of factors at once by 'adding a level'.

Finally, separate out these blocks and do a simple randomisation on each; after which you can put them back together, giving you two stratified and randomised groups.

	A	B	C	D	E
1	Delsie Backhaus	SEN	Female	White British	
2	Sarah Hickox	Not SEN	Female	White British	
3	Kono Juzaburo	SEN	Male	Asian	
4	Eleanor Keever	SEN	Female	White British	
5	Onagu Narumi	Not SEN	Female	Asian	
6	Mark Huber	Not SEN	Male	White British	
7	Jaonne Radcliff	Not SEN	Female	White British	
8	Zach McDonald	SEN	Male	White British	
9	Colin Ling	SEN	Male	Asian	
10	Erica Jones	Not SEN	Female	White British	
11	Adrian Sargent	Not SEN	Male	White British	
12	Shu Shan	Not SEN	Female	Asian	
13	Mattie Merola	SEN	Female	Asian	
14	Ebony Plank	Not SEN	Female	Asian	
15	William Morris	SEN	Male	White British	
16	etc.				
17					

Figure 4.7. Organising your data prior to stratified randomisation.

Learning Zone 4.3. Identifying factors for stratified randomisation

Go back to one of the designs that you were considering implementing from your work in the previous chapters. Think about the participants you are planning to use. What are the main characteristics that vary within this group? Think about things like gender, prior attainment and so on. Which ones do you think it might be important to control for in the randomisation process?

Remember, if you have been able to use a within-participant design this is no longer an issue, as the participants will all be acting as their own control and there is no between-participant variation.

Dealing with already stratified classes

There is one very practical variation on the approach above that we have come across in our travels around schools. Very often, primary schools (and some secondary school subject departments) will deliberately stratify classes that are blocked against each other in the timetable in order to ensure that the groups are balanced. This is particularly common in primary schools where there is two-form entry and it has been decided that the two classes should be more or less equal in terms of prior attainment, gender and so on. In this case, you can simply randomise the whole class with a single coin toss.

Although not strictly stratified randomisation, if you are confident that the two groups are more or less equal to begin with, then the approach can be similarly effective. You might call this 'random allocation of previously stratified groups'. See Brain Box 4.4 for the limitations of randomising groups of people rather than individuals.

Brain Box 4.4. The limitations of randomising groups of people rather than individuals

In all the examples so far, we have assumed that the unit of randomisation in your study is the individual participant. However, you may not be able to do this and may find yourself having to randomise at whole class or whole school level (known as cluster randomisation). If you have a within-participant design it does not really matter if you randomise at a whole class or whole school level, providing you think that any between-group variations are not going to enhance any potential carry-over effects. However, if your design is between-participant you will need to accept that there may be biases at work in your design (as a result of cluster randomisation) and interpret your results with more caution. Of course, you could improve your design if you have enough classes or schools involved by stratifying the randomisation or even case-matching the classes or schools.

Whatever you do to enhance cluster randomisation there will always be a potential design effect. However, there are some statistical approaches that can be applied to compensate for the effects of cluster randomisation. These usually involve reducing the level of significance according to the amount of bias there was in your design. There is a good explanation of one of these techniques in a free-to-download journal article by Marion Campbell, Jill Mollison, Nick Steen, Jeremy Grimshaw and Martin Eccles.[1] If you are not a maths teacher this may look scary, but ask a colleague to help once you have done your trial and calculated the basic statistics. The design effect and adjustment of significance can all be done in Excel.[2]

Pairwise randomisation

In many clinical contexts, such as surgery, psychotherapy and counselling, it is impossible to wait to recruit a large group of people and you may need to manage your resources effectively as well as conduct your research. For example, you may need to deal with people and slot them into your trial as they present with the appropriate combination of symptom and medical history.

The same situations might arise in a school if you were going to trial an intervention that was believed to reduce the number of permanent exclusions at the point at which a child reached a critical set of criteria. Alternatively, you might have an intervention that is appropriate for children

---

1 M. K. Campbell, J. Mollison, N. Steen, J. M. Grimshaw and M. Eccles, 'Analysis of cluster randomized trials in primary care: a practical approach', *Family Practice* 17 (2000): 192–196. Available at: http://fampra.oxford-journals.org/content/17/2/192.long.

2 If you can't do this remember to acknowledge cluster randomisation as a limitation in your reporting and be more cautious in your interpretation.

with a specific set of learning difficulties and profiles and know that you will need to do this over a prolonged period in order to reach the right sample size. However, you may also be aware that you will only have access to a small number of pupils at a time and limited availability with regard to the intervention. Just as a hospital might only have one or two specialist surgeons able to perform a procedure at any one time, so a school might have limited access to treatment slots delivered by educational psychologists or counsellors.

In this case there are several options. Firstly, you could recruit two participants at a time and then randomly allocate them to control or intervention at the point of enrolment. Alternatively, you could number the available treatment slots in Excel and then randomly allocate participants to control or intervention. Then, as the children 'present themselves for treatment', they would go into the predetermined (and randomised) treatment slots in the order they present.

Matched pairing or case-matching

You will recall from Chapter 3 that it is possible to have a matched pairs (or case-matched) design, in which the researcher first pairs up participants on characteristics that they share and then randomly assigns each one of the pair to a condition, so there is a balance of pupil characteristics across the control and experimental conditions.

	Gender	Reading age	Special educational needs	Random number	Allocation
John	Male	11.3	None	0.212069	Control
Abdul	Male	11.3	None	0.980547	Intervention
Tamara	Female	10.9	Dyspraxia	0.174127	Control
Shasta	Female	10.9	Dyspraxia	0.314146	Intervention
Peter	Male	10.5	None	0.966594	Intervention
Paul	Male	10.5	None	0.667341	Control
Erica	Female	9.8	Dyslexia	0.009982	Control
Joanne	Female	9.8	Dyslexia	0.774315	Intervention

Table 4.1. An example of random allocation in a matched pairs design.

For example, you might judge that reading age is important alongside gender and special educational needs. Working down your participant list child by child (see Table 4.1), you would pair them (or case-match them). In this example, you might case-match Erica and Joanne because they have the lowest reading age, are both female and are both statemented because of dyslexia. On the other hand, John and Abdul might be case-matched because they have the highest reading age, are boys and have no special educational needs. Once you have done this for all your participants, organise them as follows in Excel, produce a random number for each pair and then send the person in the pair with the lowest number to control and the one with the highest number to intervention.

Case-matching can also be very useful in situations where you can't randomise but you want to have a control group so you can improve your study's validity. In this instance, you might allocate a pool of case matches to each intervention child and then randomly sample the control group from that pool. This could happen if you were running a study on the effect of giving pupils an iPad to use at home and have to give the iPads to a certain group because of funding requirements.

If you take a look at Table 4.2 you will see how this works. Firstly, as we have already mentioned, we have case-matched each intervention child against two possible case matches – in this case, based on gender, maths attainment and history of disciplinary issues. As we know who is in the intervention, because this is a non-randomised trial, we just need to assign a random number to the two possible control condition children and then allocate the one with the highest number to control and not select the one with the lower number.

Brain Box 4.5. The concept of control

Notice how in this chapter we have been using the word 'control' more widely than just to describe the control condition that some (in a between-participant or matched pairs design) or all (in a within-participant design) participants will experience within your study – for example, you might talk about 'using stratified randomisation controlling for gender and ethnicity'.

	Name	Gender	Maths attainment	Disciplinary issues	Random number	Allocation
Possible control	George	Male	143	No issues	0.678869	Control
	Brian	Male	143	No issues	0.273648	Not selected
Intervention	Simon	Male	144	No issues	-	Intervention
Possible control	Tamara	Female	133	Occasional detention	0.897637	Control
	Shasta	Female	132	Occasional detention	0.384146	Not selected
Intervention	Jane	Female	133	Occasional detention	-	Intervention
Possible control	Paul	Male	101	Frequent detention	0.283736	Not selected
	Richard	Male	101	Frequent detention	0.93847	Control
Intervention	Taj	Male	101	Frequent detention	-	Intervention
Possible control	Erica	Female	87	At risk of exclusion	0.056982	Not selected
	Joanne	Female	88	At risk of exclusion	0.83784	Control
Intervention	Patricia	Female	88	At risk of exclusion	-	Intervention

Table 4.2. An example of random sampling from a pool of case-matched participants.

Putting your research into action

The best way of ensuring that your research is successful is to be consistent. By far the most likely thing that will have an impact on your results will be teachers and the way they deliver the protocols you have designed. Planning the content of the control condition lessons, as well as the intervention lessons, is important. Have a clear lesson plan and make sure that the teachers know what it is they are supposed to be doing.

All the details that have been described in this book so far can be brought together to produce a clear and comprehensive plan or **research protocol** for your study (i.e. a full description of the research study that can act as a sort of manual for yourself or members of your extended research team). Having a protocol means you are much more likely to complete your study and end up with some analysable results, and it is much easier if you have a structure to work with.

The next section outlines a structure that you can easily copy for use with your own research – some of the areas you will already be familiar with from the material in the first few chapters and the remainder will become clear as you work through Chapters 5 and 6.

Creating a research protocol

A research protocol will help to ensure that you keep to the methods that you decided upon when you came up with your research design. You can also use it to monitor your progress as you go from research design, to briefing anyone who is assisting you and to implementing your different conditions.

There is no fixed way to write up a research protocol, but broadly speaking it will consist of the following elements in this sort of order:

- A provisional title – which you will probably end up changing when you actually have your results.
- A summary of the purpose of the study, its background and the rationale for the project.
- A statement of your research aims.
- A statement of your hypothesis (or hypotheses if you have more than one), together with the direction of the hypothesis (whether it is one-tailed or two-tailed – a very important consideration because this will affect your results considerably). You could also include the threshold for significance that you are setting for your study (known as alpha – there is more on this in Chapter 5).

- A description of the research design – for example, is it between-participant, within-participant or matched pairs, and how many conditions (levels of the IV) will there be? It can be a good idea to draw a diagram to help explain this, like the ones we have used in earlier chapters.
- An outline of the methods that you will be using. This section will cover three areas:
  › Who the participants are going to be, the sample size (see Chapter 5) and the way in which you have randomised, assuming you are able to do so (i.e. you are not doing a quasi-experimental design).
  › The procedure you will follow – in other words, the processes that will be used both by the people who are administering the study and the participants.
  › The materials (and/or apparatus) you are going to use in your study.
- Ethical considerations.

You can also add sections covering the following areas:

- The benefits of doing the study.
- Lists of resources and costs.
- A project plan – including some dates and deadlines.

Brain Box 4.6 illustrates a short research protocol to give you an idea of the points that you might want to include in the main sections.

Brain Box 4.6. An example research protocol

Although you can end up with a very detailed research protocol, it is fine to work to a summary like the one below and then add in appendices containing all of the materials and other things that you think you need to be organised about.[3]

Provisional title	The effect of positive visualisation on the sporting performance of children
Summary (purpose, background and rationale)	There is evidence that positive visualisation, when used by professional sportspeople improves performance (Woolfolk et al., 1985).[4] Some GCSE PE syllabuses include this idea. As yet, no research has taken place that has looked at whether this is also applicable to children.
Research aims (or objectives)	• To find out whether positive visualisation improves performance in a PE lesson • To find out whether positive visualisation improves enjoyment in a PE lesson
Research design	A two-condition between-participant design will be used with a pre- and post-test. The independent variable (positive visualisation) will be operationally defined by creating two conditions: • IV level 1 (control) – Throwing 10 basketball penalty shots without coaching immediately before the shots • IV level 2 (experimental condition) – Throwing 10 basketball penalty shots with visualisation coaching immediately before the shots Dependent variables: • DV1 – Successful first throws • DV2 – Total number of baskets scored • DV3 – Enjoyment of activity using a seven-point Likert scale questionnaire

3   Note: in this example there are a couple of new statistical concepts ('power analysis' and the 'threshold for significance'), these will be explained in the next chapter.

4   R. L. Woolfolk, M. W. Parrish and S. M. Murphy, 'The effects of positive and negative imagery on motor skill performance', *Journal of Cognitive Therapy and Research* 9(3) (1985): 335–341.

Provisional title	The effect of positive visualisation on the sporting performance of children
Hypotheses (direction and threshold)	• Positive visualisation improves performance in a PE lesson focused on the basketball penalty shoot-out (one-tailed) • Positive visualisation improves enjoyment of a PE lesson focused on the basketball penalty shoot-out (one-tailed) • A threshold will be set at alpha = 0.05.
Methods: participants, sample size and randomisation	Power analysis suggests that a sample size of 156 (78 in each condition) will be needed to detect a moderate ($d = 0.04$) effect size. In order to have such a sample size, two schools will collaborate in a team science way and conduct the study in parallel with their mixed gender Year 9 pupils. Stratified randomisation will be used controlling for pupils' height, gender and whether or not they are in a school sports team.
Methods: procedure	All children will be taught to throw penalty shots prior to the experiment. Control condition children will then have a coach stood next to them while they throw who will give them general encouragement for 30 seconds before telling them to start. The experimental condition children will also be coached but will be taught a visualisation protocol involving sensory visualisation of success (visual, kinaesthetic and auditory).
Methods: materials (and apparatus)	Basketball courts and balls, script for coaches to learn, recording sheets for markers, enjoyment questionnaire.
Ethical considerations	Children will be given a consent form allowing their results to be used. Any children whose parent/guardian does not give consent will still be allowed to complete the lesson. Although children will be informed of the broad aim of exploring different coaching approaches, they will be kept blind to the full detail of the research design. However, they will be debriefed later when the results are available.

Provisional title	The effect of positive visualisation on the sporting performance of children
Appendices	Scripts Questionnaire Consent form Project plan

Table 4.3. Example of a research protocol.

Learning Zone 4.4. Drafting your research protocol

Take a few minutes to build a template like the one below in a word processing package. Begin to create a research protocol by thinking through the prompts in the right-hand column.

Provisional title	Your notes	What to include
Summary (purpose, background and rationale)		• Purpose • Background and context • Gap in the research evidence • Rationale
Research aims (or objectives)		• What you want to find out
Research design		• Type of design • Number of conditions • The tests you will use
Hypotheses (direction and threshold)		• Write your null and experimental hypothesis • Remember to include the direction of your hypothesis • State the threshold you will consider significant

Provisional title	Your notes	What to include
Methods: participants, sample size and randomisation		• Who will be the subjects of your study? • How many will you have? • Power analysis if you have done one • How will you randomise?
Methods: procedure		• What will happen in the control and intervention? • Anything else you will do to organise your research
Methods: materials (and apparatus)		• Rooms • Resources • Types of test
Ethical considerations		• Informed consent • Other ethical issues
Appendices		• A list of all the other documents you will need to create (e.g. lesson plans to brief the teachers with) and, if they request them, to help others to replicate your design

Table 4.4. Research protocol template.

Test yourself 4

Question 1

Explain what is meant by demand characteristics?

Question 2

What is the advantage of a double-blind experiment?

Question 3

What is the main disadvantage of simple randomisation?

What next?

So far in this book we have managed to avoid the mathematics associated with experiments, but we now need to look quite carefully at this. Before you begin, however, note that this is not just maths to be completed once you have your data but also to be considered before you begin your experiment. Depending on your background, the next chapter might be tricky and may introduce you to new concepts – but stick with it because quantitative experimental research without statistics is meaningless!

Chapter 5

Statistics – here comes the maths

By the end of this chapter, you will know about:

- Using descriptive and inferential statistics to analyse your data.

- How inferential tests allow you to accept or reject hypotheses.

- Using a power analysis to estimate the sample size you need.

Analysing your data – descriptive statistics

Once you have collected data from your study you need to analyse it to see if the data supports your experimental hypothesis. The first stage of this, probably best described as a preliminary analysis, requires you to calculate **descriptive statistics**. Descriptive statistics are summary values that describe your data (such as the mean, median, standard deviation and range). The type of descriptive statistics you use will be dependent on the distribution of your data (see Brain Box 5.1).

Brain Box 5.1. Data distributions

The distribution of data is a description of the data values in a data set. We usually represent distribution as a curve. The easiest way to conceptualise it is to imagine people stacked up in columns underneath the curve, with each column representing a score on your dependent variable as shown in Figure 5.1.

Our curve is bell shaped and symmetrical. We refer to a curve like this as a **normal distribution**. Certain mathematical values can be understood in terms of this curve. The mean value corresponds to the peak of the curve, while the width of the curve gives an indication of the spread of values from this mean. A wide curve would indicate a greater spread.

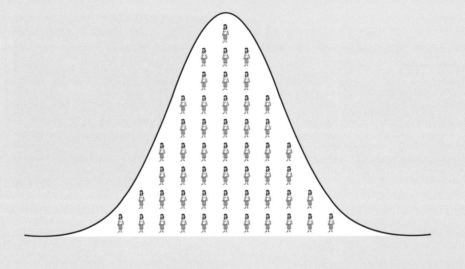

Figure 5.1. A normal distribution.

Where a data set does not give a bell-shaped curve – for example, because it is skewed to the left or right (see Figure 5.2) – it cannot be considered to have a normal distribution, so different statistical analyses and descriptions are required.

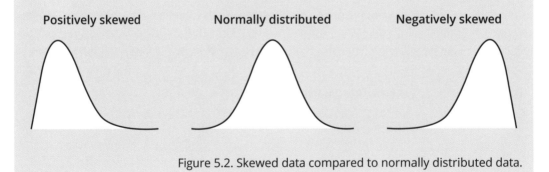

Positively skewed   **Normally distributed**   **Negatively skewed**

Figure 5.2. Skewed data compared to normally distributed data.

Mean and standard deviation

Typically, if you have normally distributed data you would report the **mean** value and the **standard deviation (SD)** for each condition. You can calculate both of these by hand but they are also very straightforward to calculate in Excel (any statistics software you use to analyse your data will produce them automatically). The mean value is the average score, while the standard deviation indicates the spread of data from this mean value – in other words, how concentrated the variation in the data is around this central point. Figure 5.3 shows two distributions with different standard deviations.

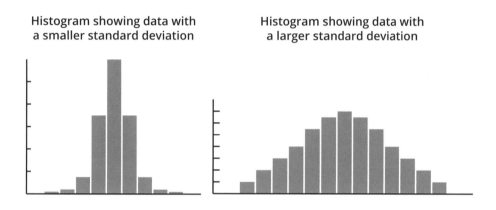

Histogram showing data with a smaller standard deviation

Histogram showing data with a larger standard deviation

Figure 5.3. Histograms showing the difference between a smaller standard deviation (left) and a larger standard deviation (right).

This could be useful information to help you interpret your findings. For example, imagine you had a dependent variable which was a maths test on which a participant could score between 0 and 100 (e.g. a percentage score). You could end up with descriptive results for a group of children like those shown in Table 5.1.

Condition	Mean score (%)	Standard deviation
Control	10	6
Intervention	45	3

Table 5.1. Hypothetical descriptive statistics.

You might conclude that the intervention not only improved attainment but also reduced the between-participant variation in scores. In other words, not only was it effective at increasing pupils' test scores, but it also facilitated a reduction in the difference between pupils within the intervention.

Standard error of the mean

Another statistic that you sometimes see reported is the **standard error of the mean** (abbreviated as SE or SEM). The best way to understand standard error is to compare and contrast it with standard deviation.

Standard deviation quantifies how much the individual scores of your participants vary, or the scatter around the mean. In contrast, standard error of the mean makes a quantitative estimate of how true your mean might be for the population you are studying. Standard error is able to do this because its formula uses both the standard deviation and the sample size. Thus, as your sample size increases so the standard error of the mean will always become smaller. In this way, standard error tells you about the reliability of your mean.

Interpreting standard error is easy. Suppose we had a mean of 34 and a standard error of 0.5. This would tell us that the true mean is likely to be between 34 plus or minus 0.5, so the true range of our mean would be between 33.5 and 34.5.

Using different descriptive statistics for different distributions

If your data is not normally distributed (i.e. it does not look like a normal distribution curve), you would usually report the **median** value. We do this for the following reason: if your data has a distribution that does not follow a bell curve (more or less), the mean does not mean very much. For example, if your data is skewed to one side the mean could be way off the central point. In such a case, the median is a better expression of the centre of the data as it represents the mid-point of the range. Likewise, standard deviation is less informative if the data is not normal and is better replaced by the **range** (i.e. the distance between the lowest and highest values).

I think you call it a paranormal distribution

Describing your data using appropriate descriptive statistics is useful, but it is not enough on its own to decide whether your hypothesis is supported or not. That requires you to make inferences from your data and to do this you must use **inferential statistics**.

Analysing your data – inferential statistics

Descriptive statistics reveal information about the average and spread of the data from your sample for the various conditions. For instance, in the example in Table 5.1, the control condition had a score of 10% while the intervention had a score of 45%. However, when we conduct experimental research, we don't just want to know about our specific sample; we also want to make 'inferences' about whether the same result would occur in the whole population in which we are interested. The way we do this is to calculate a probability value, or **p-value**, for the observed result occurring by chance. In this way, the p-value tells you the probability that the difference between your conditions could have happened by chance. This p-value indicates the **significance** of the result and is what people are referring to when they talk about 'a significant finding'.

Statistical significance

Significance is the very foundation of scientific method. Significance in science is a number; a number derived from testing which, in turn, tells you whether your result is likely to be the result of chance. From the earliest days of scientific research, it was recognised that you could easily be misled as a researcher if you assumed that the results of just one experiment were true. This is a problem because errors can and do occur. There are two types of error in particular that you should be aware of:

A **type I error** (or false positive) occurs when you make a claim that something is there when it is not (i.e. when a null hypothesis is actually true but is falsely rejected). Putting aside the very rare instances of fraud (easily detected through the inherent nature of scientific research and the processes of clear reporting and replication), these can occur for a number of reasons, including having a weak research design and not taking into account things like demand characteristics (see Chapter 4 if you have forgotten what these are).

A **type II error** (or false negative) is essentially the opposite and occurs when you have missed an effect that is really there (i.e. when a null hypothesis is actually false but is accepted). Type II errors can occur for similar reasons, but the usual reason is that you had too small a sample size.

Understanding *p*-values

Imagine if we had two people in our trial (one in the control and one in the intervention) and we tested the intervention person to see if they liked apples more after watching an advert about fruit – finding that they did indeed compared to the control person whose view did not change. We might be tempted to conclude that people like fruit more after watching the advert. How likely is it (i.e. what is the probability) that this is true for all humans? Not very, we hear you say, because we only asked two people.

OK, so what if we asked 100 people and found the same thing? Or 1,000? Well, it's getting better, isn't it? But it's not perfect – nor can it ever be. Even if we asked everyone on the planet the same question (and found everyone in the intervention having an increased positive response), we could still never be certain. This is because someone might have said the wrong thing by accident, others might have lied or at the very moment we asked the question a new person could be born who breaks the pattern of exactly 100%. An extreme example but you get the point. The same applies to any experiment, therefore we need a way of estimating or 'inferring' whether the result is significant – hence the term 'inferential test'.

P-values can only ever have a maximum value of 1 and a theoretical minimum value of 0.[1] The value $p = 1.0$ means 100% probability, while $p = 0.50$ would mean 50% probability (like tossing a coin). Following this logic, $p = 0.01$ would be a 1 in 100 probability. So how are you going to decide what threshold to consider significant? Fortunately, you have 100 years of scientific enquiry and precedent to draw on which has established $p = 0.05$ as a minimum reasonable threshold. The threshold you set in advance of your research is called **alpha** (α). Assuming that we have adopted this minimum level (alpha = 0.05), and after analysing our data the result is $p = 0.76$, we would accept our null hypothesis and state as our finding that:

> Two lessons of group work *does not improve* column addition problem-solving in a rural English primary school.

However, if we had found a *p*-value smaller than the threshold of alpha (e.g. $p = 0.03$), we would reject our null hypothesis and instead state the experimental hypothesis as our finding:

> Two lessons of groups work *improves* column addition problem-solving in a rural English primary school.

Figure 5.4 illustrates these two possibilities for our hypothetical study with *p*-levels superimposed onto two graphs.

---

1   For this reason some journal house styles will prefer you to write this value without a zero (e.g. $p = .06$).

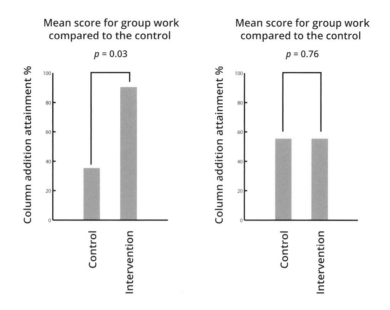

Figure 5.4. A significant finding (left) and a non-significant finding (right).

Note that when a result is not significant we actually refer to it as being 'non-significant', because it may still have meaning but not statistical significance! This raises an interesting question. Namely, what is so different about $p = 0.049$ compared to $p = 0.051$? The answer of course is not that much. Therefore, in situations where you find results that are close to your threshold, but have not crossed it (e.g. $p = 0.06$), you might adapt your interpretation of the findings accordingly. For example, you might say that the findings 'approached' significance and recommend a larger replication.[2] There is more on inferential testing in Chapter 6.

Brain Box 5.2. Using different thresholds for significance

Sometimes researchers will feel that the usually accepted minimum threshold for significance (alpha = 0.05) is just not small enough. This tends to occur where a procedure is invasive (perhaps involving injecting someone with a drug in a clinical trial) or where you are dealing with a population that is at risk (as can happen in therapy). In such cases, you may find researchers setting significance levels lower (i.e. stricter than 0.05) – for example:

   0.01 – a 1 in 100 probability that the result may have happened by chance

---

2   Again, different reviewers and journals have different opinions about using the word 'approached' in this context – so it is best to check.

0.001 – a 1 in 1,000 probability that the result may have happened by chance

In an education study, you might consider doing this if the treatment is highly controversial, expensive or involves testing children with some form of defined special educational need.

One often misunderstood thing about researcher choice regarding the threshold for significance is this: no serious scientist would ever set their alpha at a more liberal level than 0.05. Researchers only adopt different levels of significance in order to be more stringent, not less stringent – the practical implication of which is that you have to find a larger sample size.

The direction of your hypothesis and its effect on *p*-values

You will recall from Chapter 2 that hypotheses can be directional (one-tailed) or bidirectional (two-tailed). If you have a hypothesis like the one below you have set a one-tailed hypothesis because you are predicting the direction of change:

Rote learning *improves* pupils' automatic recall of their 12 times table.

However, if you had phrased it like this, you are suggesting that the result could go either way and therefore you have a two-tailed hypothesis:

Rote learning *changes* pupils' automatic recall of their 12 times table.

The type of hypothesis you have affects the *p*-value that is deemed to be significant. So far we have been making reference to the threshold alpha $= 0.05$, but this is actually the minimum accepted alpha for a two-tailed hypothesis. For a one-tailed hypothesis you need to reduce the alpha value by half in order to have the same level of stringency.

To explain why this is the case we need to explain what is meant by one-tailed and two-tailed using the idea of the distribution curve. For a one-tailed hypothesis you have made a prediction about the direction of the effect (see Figure 5.5), so only one-tail of the control curve is involved in the prediction. But for a two-tailed hypothesis both tails are involved (see Figure 5.6).

The *p*-value you report when you have set a one-tailed hypothesis is exactly half that for a two-tailed hypothesis. In other words, with exactly the same data $p = 0.07$ (two-tailed) would become $p = 0.035$ (one-tailed). This is the case because when you have a two-tailed hypothesis you are essentially 'spread betting' on two possible directions (and thus get less of a return), rather than betting everything on one direction for which you get rewarded for taking a greater risk. Something similar happens in a horse race where you can put all your money on the winner (on the nose) and get a more significant return compared to an 'each way' bet (when you spread your bet between winning and getting a second or third place) which gives a lower yield.

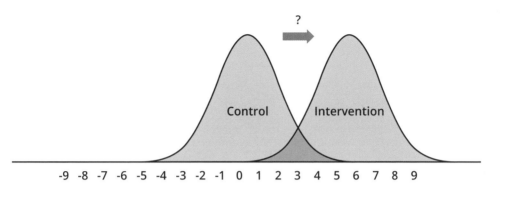

Figure 5.5. A one-tailed hypothesis.

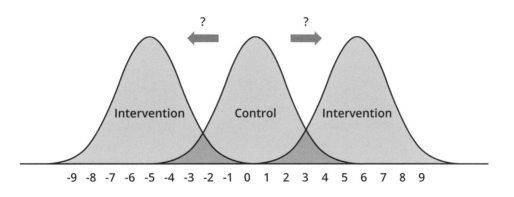

Figure 5.6. A two-tailed hypothesis.

Effect size

As well as statistical significance, another key concept is **effect size**. This statistic tells you about the strength and direction of any change that has taken place. It can therefore be a negative or positive number. For example, you might see:

$d = 0.3$

Or

$d = -0.3$

In the past, researchers tended to report the significance level (p-value) only and left it to the reader to work out the strength of the finding from other information in the paper or publication. Today, in the spirit of making findings clearer and easier to apply, it is regarded as best practice to report the effect size alongside the level of significance (e.g. $d = 0.34$, $p = 0.001$).

While we always measure significance using a probability value (e.g. $p = 0.02$), there are different measures for effect size, denoted by a variety of symbols (including d, r, ηp^2, ω, etc.). Different effect sizes have different levels of interpretation and are used in different situations. We will use the effect sizes d and r to illustrate this idea (see Table 5.2), but in Chapter 6 we will explain when to use a range of different forms.

We have already explained that the effect size tells you the strength and direction of any change. If you had an effect size of $d = 0.51$, then this would be a medium (or moderate) positive effect. For example, if your study has compared attainment in an intervention to a control condition, then the intervention has improved attainment by a moderate amount. If, on the other hand, the result had been $d = -0.51$ (notice the minus sign), then we would have a moderate negative effect on attainment. The same principle would apply to the effect size r (also illustrated in Table 5.2).

	d	r
Small	0.20	0.10
Medium	0.50	0.30
Large	0.80	0.50

Table 5.2. Interpreting the effect sizes d and r.

The terms 'small', 'medium' and 'large' were developed by a very famous statistical researcher called Jacob Cohen and relate (broadly speaking) to the notion of what you would generally expect to find in a study that has used a scientific method – assuming that the result was significant (i.e. not likely to have occurred by chance). In this way, most scientific studies might expect to find moderate results but fewer small and large effects.

At this point, you may be wondering – yes, but what does it mean? The answer to that question is nothing in and of itself. The effect size can be interpreted in two ways. Firstly, is your effect size significant or not (i.e. could it have happened by chance)? Secondly, what was the context in which it was found (i.e. the research protocol that surrounds that result (including the participants), what was done in the intervention and the control condition)? Putting effect size and significance together, you might see results like these:

d = 0.4, p = 0.04 (a medium positive effect with a 4 in 100 possibility that the result may have occurred by chance)

r = –0.05, p = 0.63 (a small negative effect with a 63 in 100 possibility that the result may have occurred by chance)

Significance and effect size are related. Whereas effect size tells you the strength and direction of change, significance is a function of effect size and sample size. In other words, significance looks at the strength of the change and combines it with the number of participants/data points in your study. For this reason, the bigger your sample size, the more likely you are to find a significant result. The final point to note is that although p-values effectively combine effect size and sample size they are non-directional, which is why it is useful to report both the effect size and the sample size.

Learning Zone 5.1. Combining effect size and significance

Take a look at the examples below. For each one decide whether the result is significant and describe the effect size using words that summarise the strength and direction of the change. We have done the first two for you in each case. You will need to use Table 5.2 to do this.

Result (alpha = 0.05)	Effect size	Significance
d = 0.32, p = 0.03	Positive moderately small effect	Significant
r = –0.78, p = 0.001	Negative large effect	Significant
d = 0.41, p = 0.43		
d = 0.02, p = 0.001		

Result (alpha = 0.01)	Effect size	Significance
r = 0.11, p = 0.02	Positive small effect	Non-significant
d = 0.83, p = 0.009	Positive large effect	Significant
r = 0.35, p = 0.04		
d = 0.67, p = 0.05		

Taking into account significance and effect size, which of all the results above would you say is most important?

Getting inside effect size

It is worth taking a moment to understand the maths behind the simplest of the effect sizes, Cohen's *d*, as it pops up in lots of education contexts – although it should be said that it is not being used correctly in many cases. Imagine if we had two studies, each with a control and an intervention, both with mean scores of 20 for control and 40 for intervention. We might be tempted to assume that these two studies each had the same effect on attainment. However, there is a lot more going on in the wonderful world of data other than the change in mean (such as the spread of the scores).

Now, suppose the distribution of scores for the two studies was as shown in Figure 5.7.

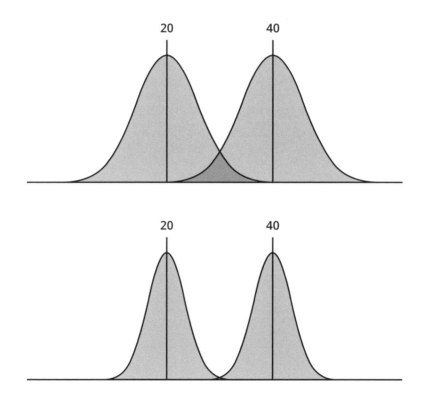

Figure 5.7. Example illustrating how two studies producing the same mean could actually have had very different effects on the participants.

In the first example, there is a lot of overlap between the data from the two conditions. That is to say, there are many children whose attainment was no different irrespective of the condition they experienced (i.e. those in the middle who share similar scores). However, in the second example, there are virtually no children with similar scores. Thus, the second study has made a much greater difference than the first (i.e. there is a stronger effect and a larger effect size).

Cohen's *d* can illustrate this with one number (e.g. *d* = 0.6) because it combines standard deviation with the mean in a basic formula that looks like this:

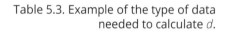

$$\text{effect size } d = \frac{\text{intervention mean} - \text{control mean}}{\text{pooled standard deviation}}$$

'Pooled' means averaged across the two conditions. For example, for the data in Table 5.3, the answer would be 0.4 (40 minus 20, divided by 50).

In the real world there is usually some degree of over-lap. An effect size of *d* = 0.8 would look something like Figure 5.8 (illustrating that there was about 47% of non-overlap, i.e. that the intervention made a clear difference for about 47% of the pupils). This does not mean, of course, that the intervention made no difference to the other pupils, many of whom will have increased their scores, but not enough to be clear of the shared area.

	Mean	Standard deviation
Control	20	50
Intervention	40	50

Table 5.3. Example of the type of data needed to calculate *d*.

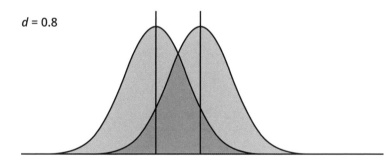

d = 0.8

Figure 5.8. Approximate overlap of scores where there is an effect size of *d* = 0.8.

d	Non-overlap
1.2	62.2%
1.0	55.4%
0.8	47.4%
0.6	38.2%
0.4	27.4%
0.2	14.8%
0.0	0%

Table 5.4. The relative amount of non-overlap for different levels of Cohen's *d*.

The approximate amount of non-overlap for different levels of Cohen's *d* is given in Table 5.4.

However, Cohen's *d* is only suitable when your data is normally distributed because it uses mean and standard deviation in its formula. If we have other types of data then we need to use other effect sizes (dz, r, ηp^2, ω or Kendall's W) – something we will return to in Chapters 6 and 7.[3]

Different inferential statistics and how they work

You may have noticed that in this chapter we have not actually told you what inferential test to conduct. There is a very good reason for this. There are many different types of test and the test you choose will depend on your design and the data you obtain (e.g. whether it has a normal distribution). Instead, for the moment, we have opted to include the general principles of inferential testing. Chapter 6 will outline the main inferential tests you need to know about to analyse the different types of design we have talked about so far. This will include the following tests, all of which are suitable for analysing the differences between two columns of data:

- Independent samples *t*-test
- Paired sample *t*-test
- Mann–Whitney *U* test
- Wilcoxon signed-rank test

We will also touch on some other tests. This will include tests suitable for situations where you have a pre- and post-test or three levels to your independent variable (which would mean having more columns of data to look at simultaneously).

Most inferential tests are now performed by entering your data into a software package. This might be as simple as entering a column of data from a control group alongside a column of data from an intervention group. To calculate the probability value (i.e. whether the difference between the two columns of data is significant), inferential tests first calculate a **test statistic**. This test statistic, when used in conjunction with the **degrees of freedom**, then produces the *p*-value. In the past, before computer programmes, researchers calculated the test statistic by hand and then looked up the *p*-value in a set of printed tables (called critical tables).

Every inferential test produces its own test statistic. The test statistic shows the amount of change that has happened according to that test. The term 'degrees of freedom' (df) refers to the number of things that are free to vary if one thing is held constant in order to provide a point of reference. Think of a football match where two goalkeepers stay in their penalty areas but the other 20 people

---

3   There are two different types of *r* in common usage, *r* used for correlation (Pearson's) and Rosenthal's *r*, which is a converted form of *d* and is used for non-normal data. They express completely different statistical concepts so make sure you use the right one.

can run round as much as they like. Usually, there are also two degrees of freedom to report, sometimes reported like this:

df = 1, 134

In most cases, the first number relates to the number of levels you have in your independent variable minus one (called the numerator), and the second number relates to the number of participants (denominator) that you have in your study in total (sometimes minus one, sometimes not, depending on the test).

Using inferential tests to assess the effects of a potential confounding variable

So far, we have assumed that you will be using inferential statistics to analyse the impact of the independent variable on the dependent variable (e.g. to determine whether your intervention scores are significantly different to your control group scores (as in Figure 5.4)). However, it is also possible to use inferential tests to assess the effects of a potential confounding variable – assuming you measured that variable.

For example, you may worry that attendance is a confounding variable in your study measuring attainment following the use of a new teaching pedagogy. You could see if there is a relationship between attendance and attainment by using inferential tests that look at the strength of the correlation. As with other types of inferential test, there are versions for normally distributed data (referred to as **parametric tests**) and versions for data that is not normally distributed (**non-parametric tests**). When it comes to correlation, the two types of statistic that you are most likely to use are:

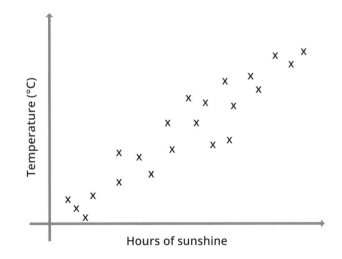

Relationship between hours of sunshine and temperature

Temperature (°C)

Hours of sunshine

- Pearson product-moment correlation coefficient (used with normally distributed interval data)

Figure 5.9. Example of a positive correlation.

- Spearman's rho (for rank ordered and non-normally distributed data)

Correlation can assess the strength of a relationship between two sets of data that are incremental – for example, the relationship between rising temperature and hours of sunshine. If both increase together this is a 'positive correlation' (see Figure 5.9).

If one increases while the other decreases, this is a 'negative correlation' – for example, the relationship between how hungry a group of people feel and how much they have eaten (see Figure 5.10).

Correlations range between 0 (no relationship) and 1 (a perfect relationship). In a perfect relationship, every data point would be in a straight line midway between the two variables. Where there is no relationship you would not be able to see any discernible pattern as the data points would be evenly spread out. The resulting data you would report would look something like this:

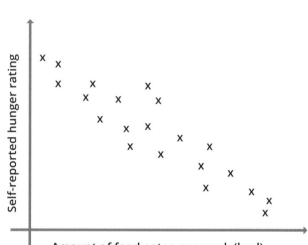

Relationship between hunger and food intake

Self-reported hunger rating

Amount of food eaten per week (kcal)

$r = 0.43, p = 0.001$

or for Spearman's rho:

$\text{rho} = 0.32, p = 0.08$

Figure 5.10. Example of a negative correlation.

As for other inferential tests, when interpreting the result you start with the p-value. This tells you if there is a significant effect or not. You then look at the effect size. With the Pearson product-moment correlation coefficient test, r^4 is the effect size as well as the test statistic and is interpreted as follows:

0.2 = small

0.5 = moderate

0.8 = large

Thus, returning to the example above, if you found no significant correlation between pupil attainment and attendance rate in either the intervention or the control, you would conclude that this had not confounded the research. However, if you found a significant correlation then there is clearly some form of association going on between these measures.

---

4   In this case this is the correlation version of r not the converted d version (as we mentioned in an earlier footnote).

Correlation does not indicate cause, just the strength of a relationship. There is always the possibility that another factor has influenced the effect – for example, as ice cream cone consumption in New York increases so does the murder rate! The causal link is an increase in temperature. This said, if there is a sound reason for correlating two variables, the statistic could be very useful indeed.

Estimating sample size before you implement your study

Statistical analyses are not just important once you have your data set but also before you collect the data. This is because you need to check that your sample size will be big enough to detect an effect, so you avoid a type II error. Performing this type of check is called a **power analysis**. There are excellent free software programmes that will help you do this (such as G*Power which is free to download from www.gpower.hhu.de/en.html).[5] We have also provided some tables and graphs that you can use for simple two-condition designs. Of course, if you see your study as a pilot or preliminary study, you may be content with a small sample size in the first instance.

G*Power allows you to enter the type of inferential statistics you are planning to use, the effect size you want to detect (or believe will be there based on prior research) and set a level of power (by convention, the minimum is considered to be 0.80 or 80%). This number corresponds to the likelihood of missing an effect because your sample is too small (i.e. a type II error). With this information, the programme will tell you what the minimum sample size is that you need.

In Table 5.5 we have given you the sample sizes that you need in order to detect an effect with two different research designs and assuming you have normally distributed data. Notice how the sample sizes are very different if you have a one-tailed or two-tailed hypothesis (because of the difference in probability value that you should report depending on this).

---

5   See also F. Faul, E. Erdfelder, A. G. Lang and A. Buchner, 'G*Power 3: a flexible statistical power analysis program for the social, behavioral, and biomedical sciences', *Behavior Research Methods* 39: 175–191.

	Effect size			
	$d = 0.2$		$d = 0.4$	
	One-tailed	Two-tailed	One-tailed	Two-tailed
Between-participant (half in control and half in intervention)	620	788	156	200
Within-participant/matched pairs	156	199	41	52

Table 5.5. Estimates of sample sizes needed to have 80% power to detect a significant effect – assuming that your threshold for significance is alpha = 0.05, you have normal data and you are comparing two conditions/groups.

To complete the picture, two graphs are shown in Figure 5.11. These illustrate the relative difference in power for a between-participant design compared with a within-participant design. From these it is easy to see the greater level of statistical power obtained depending on the design you use.

When sample sizes are too big

A second important point emerges from looking at power analysis curves like those in Figure 5.11. Beyond about 1,000 participants, the benefits of continuing to increase your sample size are negligible, with the curve ultimately flatlining at just below 0.1. Thus, if you are lucky enough to have the resources and time to go beyond 1,000 participants, you would be far better off doing a replication of a study or a series of replications. It is also the reason why many psychology studies tend to place themselves around an optimum of about 350 participants for a between-participant design. This level of scale avoids missing small effects and at the same time avoids ending up with the interpretative challenge of a tiny significant effect size that is probably more due to sample size rather than anything important that is occurring in the real world.

Building sample sizes in school-based experimental research through collaboration

As we have seen, building a reasonable sample size is a good idea – providing you don't do it just to be able to claim a small effect as significant. There are various ways this can be achieved in a school setting.

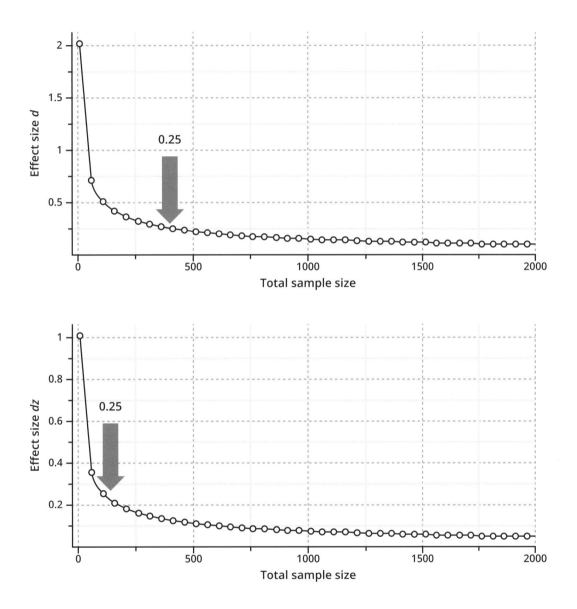

Figure 5.11. Graphs showing the relationship between the effect size (able to be detected as significant) and sample size for a between-participant design (top) and a within-participant design (bottom), both with alpha = 0.05, one-tailed and 80% power.

Think team science

In the context of school-based experimental research, a great way to increase your sample size is to take a 'team science' approach. Team science is a way of working that has become the latest exciting development in a wide range of scientific fields. In this approach, teams collaborate at different trial sites in order to pool their skills and build a larger sample size.

In an education context, to avoid between-school variation across control or intervention, it is beneficial to have both control and intervention groups in each of the school sites that contribute participants. In this way, you can easily get to a sample size in excess of 200 pupils.

Think like Darwin

A further possible solution is just to take the long view by planning to do your research in phases over several years. Charles Darwin spent many years collecting samples until the extent of his collection and notes was sufficient to establish his theory. In the same way, if you have a particular three week approach that you usually use in the first term with Year 7 pupils, but you know you will only have access to two classes a year (60 participants in total), you might decide to do your research over three years, amalgamating the results over time. This would then give you 180 participants in your study after three years.

Brain Box 5.3. Building sample size by collaborating across a number of schools

James Siddle completed one of the first teacher-led randomised controlled trials as part of the Department for Education/National College for Teaching and Leadership programme Closing the Gap: Test and Learn. He looked at the effect of verbal and visual-digital feedback on creative writing compared to written feedback. The approach he took demonstrates the power of collaboration across schools to build sample size.

His study was between-participant with the intervention lasting for one week only. By working collaboratively, pooling pupils from 11 classes and 10 primary schools, he was able to have a sample size of 231 pupils (120 boys and 111 girls). This sample enabled him to detect significant effect sizes not only for the whole group of participants but also for subgroups, such as boys, pupils with free school meals and pupils with special educational needs.[6]

---

6   You can read James Siddle's research report in Churches and McAleavy, *Evidence That Counts*.

Think like a surgeon

An additional possibility is to do what some research into surgery does by using a form of 'pairwise randomisation' (as discussed in Chapter 3). The problem in surgery is a practical one: in many cases, surgical interventions cannot be put on hold while a large enough sample is recruited. The answer is to randomise the treatment slots in advance of having any patients. The patients then go into the treatment slots as they present themselves for treatment.

In a school context, it might work in the following way. In one school where Richard worked, he was asked by the head teacher to be the head of house temporarily as they had a vacancy. Richard had previously led the pastoral team as part of a senior management role in another school. This particular school, a large comprehensive in the south-east of London, had four houses and a disciplinary system in which heads of subject could send students to the heads of house room at the end of the day if they had broken rules. Heads of house then had the option to put the children on report (which involved every lesson and every day being signed off by teachers and parents and a return to the heads of house room at the end of each day). As the option was always there to apply 'zero tolerance' or to give a 'final warning' instead, Richard always wondered (and still does to this day) which was the best course of action.

By adopting the approach you might apply to surgery, what he could have done was to randomly allocate 200 treatment slots to either a control or intervention (the control being 'final warning' and the intervention 'on report straight away') (see Table 5.6).

The first child in the queue at the end of the first day would get the control, the second the intervention and so on. Once he reached 200 (100 in the control and 100 in the intervention) he could have stopped and done his analysis. Bearing in mind the numbers that used to show up (particularly on a Friday) this would not have taken too long!

For his dependent variable, he could have adopted a number of measures, such as:

- Number of days before they were in trouble again in class.
- Attendance and punctuality.
- Detentions.
- Class effort grades.

Treatment slot	Condition
1	Control
2	Intervention
3	Control
4	Control
etc.	Intervention

Table 5.6. Random allocation of treatment slots for a trial where participants will be presenting themselves for treatment one at a time.

Test yourself 5

Question 1

Describe in words the following descriptive data that results from a study:

Condition	Mean maths score (%)	Standard deviation
Normal classroom practice	64	10
Peer marking practice	69	20

Question 2

What does a *p*-value of 0.02 mean for a two-tailed hypothesis?

Question 3

What is power analysis?

What next?

You have now acquired a grounding in the core statistical concepts that you will need to analyse your data. In the next chapter, we will focus on inferential testing – the process that will enable you to calculate *p*-values.

Chapter 6

A basic introduction to the most frequently used inferential statistics

By the end of this chapter you will know about:

- The basic principles of inferential testing so you can begin to learn how to calculate *p*-values for your studies.
- The names of the most frequently used inferential tests.
- How you might apply these tests to the sort of between-participant, within-participant and matched pairs designs we have covered in this book.

What is and what is not in this chapter

This chapter introduces the principles that apply to analysing data with inferential tests so you can produce the *p*-value that will tell you whether you have a significant result or not. Statistical analysis is a topic in itself and would take several books to cover in its entirety. The level of detail we go into here is suitable for reporting straightforward experimental and quasi-experimental designs in informal contexts such as school improvement projects. You should also be aware that the tests we discuss have many other uses. The aim is not to give you a comprehensive guide but rather to provide a brief outline of some of the ways that you could analyse data from the types of teacher-led research we have discussed so far. If you want to conduct a more complicated analysis, publish in academic journals or use more complex designs than the ones we have discussed in the preceding chapters, you will need to extend your reading.

Firstly, you will need to identify some software that can do the analysis for you. Every type of software has its own ways of working, so you will need a suitable manual or other guidance in order to learn how to apply the various tests correctly. Online tests and Excel spreadsheets are also available; however, be cautious when selecting them. Many online tests (and free spreadsheets) are fine to use and produce accurate results, but check that they originate from a reputable provider.

The standard software package used by most universities is an IBM product called SPSS (Statistical Package for the Social Sciences), but there are others (like SAS, R and Matlab). If you attend any of the training that Richard delivers or has designed, you will have access to Excel spreadsheets which do all of the tests we describe below, as well as the assumption testing (more about this later).

If you want to take your learning beyond this book to degree and postgraduate level, we highly recommend:

Julie Pallant, *SPSS Survival Manual: A Step by Step Guide to Data Analysis Using IBM SPSS*, 5th edn (Maidenhead: Open University Press, 2013).

Another commonly used book covering highly advanced concepts is:

Andy Field, *Discovering Statistics Using IBM SPSS Statistics*, 4th edn (London: SAGE, 2013).

Extending your reading to books like these will also introduce you to designs where you have multiple independent variables with several levels (factorial designs) and sophisticated ways to analyse data from observational studies, as well as experiments and quasi-experiments.

How this chapter is organised

This chapter is organised in the following way. Firstly, we will explain how you might use inferential tests on data from designs with two levels to the independent variable and just a post-test – for example, a design in which participants are exposed to two conditions (a control and an intervention) and where measurement only takes place after treatment. We begin with these types of design because they are the simplest to deal with. This will give you a grounding in the core principles involved. We will then go on to look at the most straightforward options you have with a pre- and post-test design, and then move on to the additional testing you will need to source when you have three levels to your independent variable – for example, if you tested two interventions at once against a control condition.

The chapter also includes a discussion about outliers (scores you find that are beyond any normally expected distribution) and the conventions with regard to dealing with them. Each section will include a table showing the type of data you can analyse with the inferential tests we discuss, so you can be clear about what you will be aiming to produce from your design and understand how to keep your data organised. It is easy to get in a muddle with your data, so having some models of how to organise it can be helpful.

We are only going to discuss the inferential testing that you are likely to need to use – the testing that produces the *p*-value. You will also need to calculate the effect size and report descriptive statistics – such as the mean and standard deviation (areas we began discussing in the last chapter and will continue to explore in the final chapter on interpretation and reporting). Excel has easy-to-use options for calculating things like the mean, median and standard deviation. There are also many websites where you can calculate effect sizes from this type of data or from the results of inferential tests.

Designs with two levels to the independent variable and a post-test only

If you have two levels to your independent variable and a post-test only design, for each dependent variable you are going to end up with some columns of data (like the examples in Tables 6.1, 6.2 and 6.3). Table 6.1 illustrates data from a between-participant design with two levels to the independent variable (control and intervention). You would end up with similar data if you had a quasi-experimental design (e.g. one that compared the response of boys and girls to the same treatment).

In the tables below, we have included pretend student names so you can see the concept more clearly, but remember that data should always be anonymised. We recommend using ID numbers or codes (as discussed in Chapter 1).

Name	Control	Name	Intervention
Dwain Arocho	4.02	Porsha Muriel	4.00
Nana Swink	4.24	Daryl Virgil	14.16
Eleanora Sheller	6.45	Dorris McCullers	4.40
Alvera Toto	9.54	Joe Neel	4.00
Chauncey Keegan	4.84	Marianne Loftis	6.20
Fredia Bradish	4.96	Becki Williams	2.02
Hattie Christie	3.74	Ileana Kearley	4.00
Ingeborg Strub	6.20	Deirdre Rael	8.40

Table 6.1. Example data from a between-participant (post-test only) design with two levels to the independent variable.

Table 6.2 shows data from a similar but within-participant design, and Table 6.3 shows data from a matched pairs design.

Name	Order in which the two conditions were experienced	Control	Intervention
Chung Hampson	Control → Intervention	4.3	6.5
Dino Lord	Control → Intervention	6.4	4.3
Shauna Dennehy	Control → Intervention	4.1	6.7
Hyon Pennington	Control → Intervention	3.2	4.3
Carolee McDavis	Intervention → Control	4.3	4.3
Ilana Allan	Intervention → Control	2.2	6.9
Margie Linnen	Intervention → Control	3.4	7.6
Ivette Thakkar	Intervention → Control	4.3	4.4

Table 6.2. Example data from a counterbalanced within-participant (post-test only) design with two levels to the independent variable.

Depending on the software that you use to do your inferential testing, your data will need to be organised in different ways. For within-participant and matched pairs data, you will need to keep a careful track of which participants did what and usually you will need to organise the data horizontally for each participant or pair (as in Tables 6.2 and 6.3). Check any guidance that comes with the software so you know exactly how to enter your data to get the right result.

	Name	Control	Name	Intervention
Pair 1	Rema Espana	59.6	Ute Roldan	51.0
Pair 2	Kathaleen Nestle	56.3	Merlene Thong	41.3
Pair 3	Jen McClary	34.8	Robbie Feldt	57.5
Pair 4	Queenie Bach	37.5	Beula Rhodus	50.0
Pair 5	Retha Grajales	36.3	Freeman Levingston	61.3
Pair 6	Tressie Ruppert	37.0	Cedrick Christensen	36.0

Table 6.3. Example data from matched pairs design with two levels to the independent variable.

When it comes to reporting, the simplest way to express the types of data above is in a bar chart, like the one in Figure 6.1. For basic school improvement reporting, this would be suitable for all of the different designs above and is a style of chart that most people can easily read and understand.

In the example below, we have chosen to show a bar chart for a quasi-experimental study. The p-value has been superimposed to show the difference we are seeking to assess using an inferential test. To recap what we have learned already: assuming that we were looking for the usual threshold for significance (a p-value of less than $p = 0.05$), and in this case as the p-value is less than that ($p = 0.001$), we would conclude that maths attainment of the girls was indeed higher than that of the boys.

Remember to check if the software has produced the one-tailed or two-tailed p-value and use the correct one depending on your hypothesis (as explained in Chapter 5).

Once you have organised your data you are going to have to work out which type of inferential test is the right one to use to analyse your results and work out what the p-value is for your study. If you have more than one dependent variable (e.g. if you measured maths attainment with a standardised test and classroom confidence using a Likert scale), you will need to do a separate analysis on the results for each dependent variable.

Every type of inferential test has assumptions (or rules) you need to meet in order to use that test. There are different tests that are suitable for between-participant designs compared to within-participant or matched pairs designs. In addition, some tests are suitable for interval data and others for ordinal data. There are also special tests for nominal (or categorical) data. Finally, some tests make assumptions about the type of distribution (e.g. whether the data is normally distributed or not) and some require other assumptions to be met, such as equal variance (we will explain what this means later).

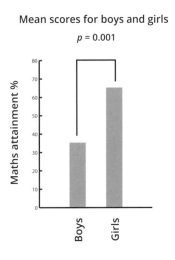

Mean scores for boys and girls

$p = 0.001$

Figure 6.1. A bar chart illustrating results from a study with two levels to the independent variable.

Types of data in focus

As we've seen, different inferential tests are suitable for different types of data. The three types of data you need to be clear about are interval data, ordinal data and nominal (or categorical) data, which we first encountered in Chapter 2.

Interval data

Interval data is data that comes from the use of scales from which you know the order of results and the exact difference between scores. For example, if we measured people's heights using centimetres then we would know who was tallest and shortest and what the exact difference was between them. In a school context, the overall average score on a classroom test with multiple questions is interval data. Other types of interval data could include:

- A standardised reading age score.
- Teacher classroom tests of various sorts which involve adding up the marks given to a number of questions based on a mark scheme (as in past GCSE or SATs papers).

Ordinal data

Ordinal data is data which comes from the use of rank ordering. With ordinal data, although we know the order of the results, we do not know what the exact differences are between them. Looking again at the question of people's heights, instead of using a tape measure we could apply our subjective judgement to rank order the people from tallest to shortest. In this case, we would still know who was tallest and shortest but we would not know exactly by how much they differed. Likert scales, where people rate their subjective perception in response to something, are also ordinal. For example:

I feel uncomfortable   1   2   3   4   5   6   7   I feel comfortable

Another example could occur if you decided to have one person marking your test who acts as a single fair tester (i.e. blind to who was in control and intervention), and you asked them to rank order the children's work across control and intervention (as in Table 6.4).

In this case, to facilitate a clearer result, the researcher has given the marker the instruction to have no tied ranks.

Name	Control	Name	Intervention
Delsie Backhaus	1	Hyacinth Soucie	9
Vasiliki Hickox	2	Maricruz Owen	16
Eric Krauss	14	Lawrence Pounders	18
Elinor Keever	10	Kay Siple	6
Delta Lacey	3	Maia Lupton	17
Fleta Huber	19	Carman Cribbs	20
Ashly Kirsh	4	Benedict Overfield	11
Zachery McPheeters	5	Clorinda Autin	15
Chrystal Hackett	8	Porsche Bischoff	7
Meri Larrison	12	Francesco Hayhurst	13

Table 6.4. Example of rank ordering across a control and intervention in a between-participant design with two levels to the independent variable.

Nominal (or categorical) data

Nominal data occurs when you have counted the number of things that fit into a category. In a school context, this type of data could be passes or fails, as is illustrated in Table 6.5 (or perhaps the number of days of exclusion before and after an initiative was introduced which aimed to reduce these). This type of table is called a contingency table.

	Passes	Fails
Control	62	140
Intervention	132	59

Table 6.5. Example of a contingency table illustrating data from a post-test only study with two levels to the independent variable.

Learning Zone 6.1. Types of data in the studies you are considering

Go back to the designs you have been thinking about during earlier sections of this book. Look again at your dependent variable(s) and identify what type of data you are going to be using.

The tests that are usually used for a post-test only design with two levels to the independent variable

The inferential tests most commonly used when you have two columns of data that you want to compare are as follows:

- Independent samples *t*-test (also known as the 'student *t*-test')
- Paired sample *t*-test
- Mann–Whitney *U* test
- Wilcoxon signed-rank test

Although tests like these can sound a bit strange, this is often just because they take the name of the person (or people) who first designed them (such as Frank Wilcoxon who came up with the Wilcoxon signed-rank test in 1945). However, all inferential tests produce the *p*-values you are after.

The independent samples *t*-test is suitable for between-participant designs where you have interval data (see page 100). It is a parametric test and is therefore suitable only for data that is normally distributed (i.e. it looks like a bell curve). If you need to, review Chapter 5 for the discussion on normal distribution.

Figure 6.2. A distribution that looks like a bell, indicating that the data is most likely normally distributed.

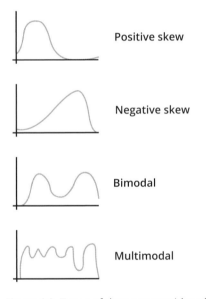

Figure 6.3. Types of data not considered to represent a normal distribution.

The distribution needs to be checked for each column of data. You can check if you have a normal distribution in a variety of ways, including constructing a histogram or doing a formal test, such as a Kolmogorov–Smirnov test or D'Agostino–Pearson test (also known as D'Agostino's K2 test), or, if your software will allow, by looking at what are called P-P and Q-Q plots. The Kolmogorov–Smirnov and D'Agostino–Pearson tests produce a *p*-value which assesses if the distribution is normal or not. P-P and Q-Q plots are graphs that show patterns within the data and which can add another level of assessment.

If your data does not look normally distributed, and the shape of the histogram is more like any of the distributions in Figure 6.3, you cannot use the independent samples *t*-test. Instead, you would need to use its non-parametric equivalent – the Mann–Whitney *U* test.

Data can also move away from normality by looking a bit squashed, even though it has a sort of bell shape. We call this aspect of distribution kurtosis (see Figure 6.4).

Mesokurtic
(normal distribution)

Leptokurtic

Platykurtic

Figure 6.4. Types of kurtosis.

In contrast to the independent samples *t*-test, although suitable only for between-participant data, the Mann–Whitney *U* test does not care what your initial distribution is like because it begins by changing your data into rank orders before comparing these rank orders for each level of your independent variable. For this reason, if you have ordinal data and a between-participant design, you would choose the Mann–Whitney *U* test. Brain Box 6.1 explains more about the independent samples *t*-test and why you may need to switch to its alternative, the Mann–Whitney *U* test, depending on the extent to which you have violated any assumptions.

Brain Box 6.1. The main assumptions of the independent samples *t*-test

The main assumptions and rules you need to apply to use the independent samples *t*-test can be summarised as follows:

- You have two columns of data with a more or less equal number of participants in each (more than a 5% difference, approximately, would usually be considered unequal, although there is no exact rule for this).
- Your design was between-participant.
- Your dependent variable produces interval data.
- Your data is normally distributed.
- There is equal variance (also known as homogeneity of variance) between the two columns of data.

You can test for the last assumption (equal variance) using a test called Levene's test, in which case you look for a non-significant result, as a significant result would suggest that the variances are different. Variance is the spread, or dispersion, of the scores and is related to the standard deviation. This said, check your software manual or guidance carefully for anything else that may be required to make the test function correctly.

If you do not meet any of the assumptions required, you need to use the Mann–Whitney *U* test instead. There is, however, a version of the independent samples *t*-test that can cope with unequal variance as long as you meet the other assumptions. If you cannot access this version of the *t*-test, it is acceptable to use the Mann–Whitney *U* test instead.

The independent samples *t*-test and Mann–Whitney *U* test are the two tests you need when you end up with two columns of between-participant data (as in Table 6.1). If your study uses a within-participant design or a matched pairs design, you will end up with two columns of data like the data in Tables 6.2 and 6.3, in which case you will need to use another inferential test. This will be either the paired sample *t*-test or the Wilcoxon signed-rank test. You guessed it: one is the parametric test and the other is the non-parametric test.

The paired sample *t*-test is the test you use when you have normally distributed interval data and the Wilcoxon signed-rank test is the non-parametric alternative, which is used when your data is not normally distributed or when the data is ordinal. Just like the Mann-Whitney *U* test, the Wilcoxon signed-rank test starts by turning everything into ranks – hence its name. There is one slight difference however: the paired sample *t*-test does not care about equal variance because the two columns of data you are using belong to the same people, or people that you are considering to be similar enough to count as such (in the case of a matched pairs design).

A last possibility occurs if you have nominal (or categorical) data. If this is the case, whatever your design, you will need to source a form of chi-squared test. There are several types of chi-squared test and different ways of using them.

Brain Box 6.2. The assumptions you need to meet to use a paired sample *t*-test

The first point to make about the paired sample *t*-test and its non-parametric alternative, the Wilcoxon signed-rank test, is this: neither of these statistics tests will function if you do not have, for each participant or matched pair, all the scores for all the levels of the independent variable you have measured. In other words, if one of your participants (or member of a matched pair) completed just the control or just the intervention, then you will have to drop that participant/pair from the study. This said, if you have a reasonably large sample and the amount of missing data is small, it is considered acceptable by some commentators to replace the missing data with the mean for the column of data where there is a missing score. However, you must explain this in your report and expect to have to justify it. When people drop out of your study the name for this is participant attrition – and it can cast doubt on the validity of your results if your attrition rates are too high.

You also need to maintain your data carefully as any software you use will expect you to be able to enter it in a way which indicates that a single participant did both conditions, or which allows for the pairing of participants in a matched pairs design to be included in the analysis. Usually, as we noted above, you organise the data horizontally to show the participant or pairing.

The main assumptions that your data needs to meet for you to be able to use the paired sample *t*-test are:

- You have two columns of data with no missing data in either of the columns.

- Your design was within-participant or matched pair.
- Your dependent variable produces results that would be classed as interval data.
- Your data is normally distributed.

There is no need to check for equity of variance with this test. Again, examine your software manual or guidance carefully for anything else that may be required to make the test function correctly.

Summary of the inferential tests we have told you about so far

Pooling together all of the principles and assumptions we have discussed gives us a map of which inferential test to use when you have two levels to your independent variable (see Figure 6.5 – this only refers to the tests we have discussed).

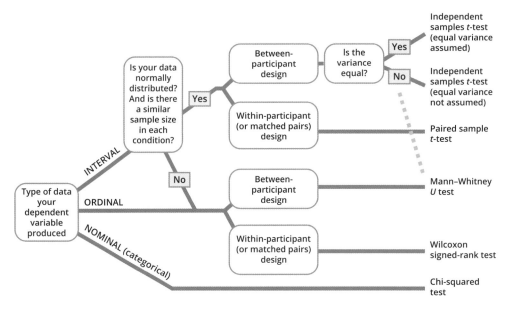

Figure 6.5. When to use the tests we have discussed so far in this chapter.

There other tests you can use for these same situations. You can find out about them in the sort of statistics books we referred to earlier.

Learning Zone 6.2. Converting classroom data to make it suitable for analysis

As a teacher, you will often want to make use of data that is not currently numerical or may need further adaptation to make it suitable for inferential testing. The two commonest situations where this occurs are when you have data that is organised alphabetically and when you have figures that look like they contain decimal places but in fact don't.

If you have data which is alphabetical, such as the exam grades A*, A, B, C, D, E, F, G, U, this will need to be converted to numbers before it can be analysed. If you need to do this, think about which letter you consider to be the high score. Your data will be much easier to deal with, in the case above, if you convert A* to 9 rather than 1.

A second situation to watch out for is where you have decimal places in your grade book that are not really decimal places. This happens frequently in England where, over a number of years, schools sub-levelled national curriculum levels (e.g. 1.1, 1.2, 1.3, 2.1, 2.2, 2.3). The intention was that the step from 1.3 to 2.1 is equal in distance travelled from step 1.1 to 1.2. Although this might be OK if everyone in the school understands it, mathematically this is problematic; any software you use for inferential testing will see 1.3 to 2.1 as a greater leap up the scale than the change from 1.1 to 1.2. Therefore, you will need to convert this form of assessment to a scale with equal sequential steps (e.g. 1 to 6). The same applies to sub-levelling with a combination of numbers and letters (e.g. 1a, 1b, 1c, 2a, 2b, 2c). These types of data contain both the problems described above so they will also need to be converted.

Have a look at the types of data that you use in your school and classroom grade book and think about the sorts of things that you might want to use as a dependent variable in a study. Which ones are immediately suitable for inferential testing because they are numerical and sequential, and which ones would require conversion?

Pre- and post-test designs with two levels to the independent variable

In the last section, we covered what to do when you end up with two columns of data because you had either a between-participant design or a within-participant design with just a post-test. Adding in a pre-test has advantages. However, a pre-test creates complexity in your design because you now end up with double the number of columns of data on which you ideally want to do a single inferential test. For example, you might end up with between-participant data that looks like Table 6.6 or within-participant data like Table 6.7.

Name	Control		Name	Intervention	
	Pre-test	Post-test		Pre-test	Post-test
Leta Cooksey	292	364	Lady Willert	272	352
Shera Rather	328	328	Bradley Hennemann	320	324
Alvin Violet	252	312	Arlyne Absher	288	308
Taunya Toups	184	276	Kayla Flores	240	236
Wanda May	336	252	Angel Kampa	272	288
Tierra Tso	304	388	Merna Lafontaine	316	332
Tia Brickley	360	332	Argelia Brabham	324	352
Mackenzie Muench	304	308	Takisha Rexford	328	324
Mee Prada	116	240	Kasey Bulfer	288	308

Table 6.6. Pre- and post-test between-participant data from a study with two levels to the independent variable.

Name	Order in which the conditions were experienced	Control		Intervention	
		Pre-test	Post-test	Pre-test	Post-test
Vi Astin	Control → Intervention	232	248	284	276
Landon Etherton	Control → Intervention	328	384	312	352
Jasmine Berkman	Control → Intervention	292	312	268	352
Renate Hayton	Control → Intervention	328	316	332	332
Donny Shoener	Intervention → Control	252	276	340	304
Sue Nold	Intervention → Control	184	248	352	376
Tennie Rettig	Intervention → Control	336	308	368	404
Birdie Cogar	Intervention → Control	304	348	328	380

Table 6.7. Example of pre- and post-test (counterbalanced) within-participant data from a study with two levels to the independent variable.

Having this type of data means that you can produce a graph to explain the data, which will look something like the example in Figure 6.6.

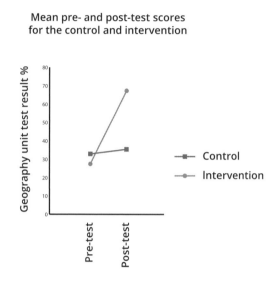

Figure 6.6. A line graph summarising the type of data illustrated in Tables 6.6 and 6.7.

Calculating the *p*-value in a pre- and post-test design where you have two levels to the independent variable

The three simplest options you have for analysing all four columns of data in this type of design are as follows (however, there are other ways to do it):

- Calculate gain scores – this will reduce your data to two columns, after which you can do one of the inferential tests you have already learned about.

- ANCOVA (analysis of covariance) – this is a form of inferential test that can deal with multiple columns of data at once.

- Conduct separate inferential tests across the pre-test data and then across the post-test data, comparing the two *p*-values for these tests.

Which of these options you choose will depend on both the nature of your hypothesis and what you can do, bearing in mind any assumptions you need to meet.

Analysing pre- and post-test data with gain scores

A gain score is the difference between the post-test score and the pre-test score. You calculate gain scores by subtracting the pre-test score from the post-test score for each participant. Table 6.8 illustrates how this would work with regard to the data in Table 6.6.

Name	Control		Gain score	Name	Intervention		Gain score
	Pre-test	Post-test			Pre-test	Post-test	
Leta Cooksey	292	364	72	Lady Willert	272	352	80
Shera Rather	328	328	0	Bradley Hennemann	320	324	4
Alvin Violet	252	312	60	Arlyne Absher	288	308	20
Taunya Toups	184	276	92	Kayla Flores	240	236	-4
Wanda May	336	252	-84	Angel Kampa	272	288	16
Tierra Tso	304	388	84	Merna Lafontaine	316	332	16
Tia Brickley	360	332	-28	Argelia Brabham	324	352	28
Mackenzie Muench	304	308	4	Takisha Rexford	328	324	-4
Mee Prada	116	240	124	Kasey Bulfer	288	308	20

Table 6.8. Reducing the data from a pre- and post-test design to two columns of gain scores.

Having calculated the gain score for each participant, you then check whether the necessary test assumptions are met for the two columns of gain scores – as you would do for a statistical test with just post-test scores. Then you carry out the appropriate inferential test to produce a single p-value (independent samples t-test, paired sample t-test, Mann–Whitney U test or Wilcoxon signed-rank test).

There are a couple of things to say about gain scores. Firstly, they have caused a lot of spilled ink over the years as some people are less keen on using them than others. However, the key point is that they are OK to use as long as you change your hypothesis to be about 'progress' rather than 'attainment' – a point well made by Jacob Cohen who created Cohen's d. If this shift in language is good enough for him, then we think the rest of us can be reasonably content about it. The reason for this is that by using gain scores, you end up comparing the relative angle of the slopes between pre- and post-test scores in response to each condition rather than the actual data points.

In fact, if your hypothesis states 'progress' as the area you are interested in testing, as Cohen suggests you can argue for the use of gain scores right from the start. It is also possible to use another test – a one-way ANOVA (analysis of variance) to analyse two columns of data containing gain scores – an approach some commentators prefer.

Analysing pre- and post-test data with ANCOVA

The second option is to use an inferential test called ANCOVA. ANCOVA stands for analysis of covariance. A covariant is an additional variable that you add into an analysis that you want to be taken into account when analysing your dependent variable. In the case of a two-condition pre- and post-test design, using ANCOVA allows all four columns of data to be analysed at once while producing one overall p-value (a concept illustrated in Figure 6.7).

Depending on the software you use, you will need to enter the data in different ways but you will always label the pre-test as the covariant and the post-test as the dependent variable in the analysis. When used in this way, ANCOVA essentially answers the question: are the post-test scores different, bearing in mind the relative starting point of each participant as measured by their pre-test score?

The main challenge with ANCOVA is that it has a number of very tricky to meet and challenging assumptions that you must test for (including what are known as homogeneity of regression slopes and homoscedasticity of residuals). These are beyond the scope of this book, but are well-documented online and always explained in software manuals and related statistics books. This said, there are also non-parametric forms of ANCOVA (such as Quade's F, which is far less fussy but not so widely available). The important point to remember is that, as with all inferential tests,

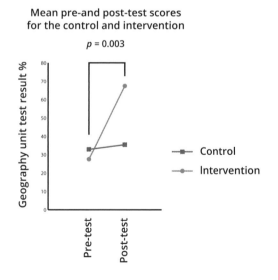

Figure 6.7. How ANCOVA can analyse the difference between post-test scores, taking into account people's starting point (the pre-test).

you should never use ANCOVA unless you are sure you have met all the assumptions because the formula just will not work properly without them and you can end up being very misled by the result.

Analysing pre- and post-test data using separate tests

Another simple option is to do separate tests comparing pre-test scores on the control and intervention (see Figure 6.8) to see if the difference is significant, and then to do the same thing on post-test scores. In the case of Figure 6.8, if the first test was not significant ($p = 0.42$) but the second was significant ($p = 0.01$), we would conclude that the intervention had made a difference.

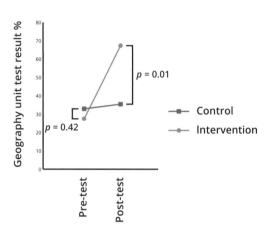

Mean pre- and post-test scores for the control and intervention

Figure 6.8. Conducting separate tests on pre- and post-test data.

Brain Box 6.3. An example of how one teacher used a 2 x 2 chi-squared test of independence with a pre- and post-test design

You may want to use nominal (or categorical) data within a pre- and post-test design. One simple way to do this is shown below. Two contingency tables were first constructed from the results (see Tables 6.9 and 6.10). Data in the tables suggested that children enjoyed maths more in the lessons that started with Mind Gym.

	Pre-test	Post-test
Enjoyed the learning	10	14
Did not enjoy the learning	20	16

Table 6.9. Contingency table showing the number of control group children enjoying maths before and after treatment.

	Pre-test	Post-test
Enjoyed the learning	10	28
Did not enjoy the learning	20	2

Table 6.10. Contingency table showing the number of intervention group children enjoying maths before and after treatment.

A chi-squared test of independence indicated a significant improvement in enjoyment during the Mind Gym lesson ($p = 0.001$), a large effect size ($\omega = 0.62$). However, there was no difference in the control group ($p = 0.45$).[1]

Learning Zone 6.3. Find a test and see what happens when you use it

Here are a series of tasks that will help you to see that different tests will produce different results.

1　Open your web browser and find an online test. Search by typing in something like 'online Mann–Whitney U test'. Alternatively, a good place to find a range of tests is a website called Social Science Statistics (www.socscistatistics.com).

2　Follow the instructions and enter some pretend data – you could use some of the example data we have given you in tables above. Find the p-value and see what it says. Change the data and see what happens next.

3　Copy and paste the data to double the amount of data, so you can see how the p-value will become smaller when you have a larger sample size. Remember to also source the functions you need to do assumption testing (such as a histogram builder and Levene's test).

4　Have a go at using the same data with different tests and see how this affects the results. In general, the parametric tests will be more sensitive and therefore more likely to detect a significant result, although this may not always be the case – it will depend on your distributions.

5　Finally, you could search online for some 'effect size calculators' so you can see the sort of data you are going to need to have if you want to use them.

1　Thanks to Danielle Kingham for permission to use these tables.

Different effect sizes for different situations

If you did the final activity in Learning Zone 6.3 and searched for effect size calculators, you will probably have noticed that there were many different types of effect size (as we stated in Chapter 5, although we focused on just two of them there). Just as different types of design and data are suitable for different inferential tests, so too with effect size – the measure that tells you the strength and direction of the change (see Chapter 5 if you need to review this).

The main ones you are likely to want to use, and the usual way to apply them and interpret them, can be found in Table 6.11. Different journals and textbooks occasionally have different views on this, so check the expectations of any publication you are intending to write for. For example, in relation to d, some people argue that this is really only suitable for between-participant data, so if you have within-participant data you should use dz instead (an effect size which takes into account any relationship between the two columns of data). This said, most people tend to use d for both.

Designs with three levels to the independent variable

If there are three levels to your independent variable, you will need to use more complicated statistics and approaches in order to analyse your data. For example:

    IV level 1 (control condition) – Continued support in class

    IV level 2 (intervention A) – Withdrawn from class for 30 minutes a week without structured scheme of work

    IV level 3 (intervention B) – Withdrawn from class for 30 minutes a week with the structured scheme of work in place

A between-participant design with three levels to the independent variable might produce data like that illustrated in Table 6.12, and a within-participant design data similar to that in Table 6.13.

Interpretation	Between two levels of an independent variable			Across three levels of an independent variable using ANOVA		Different types of ANCOVA
	Normally distributed interval data	Non-normal interval data and ordinal data	Category data	Normally distributed interval data	Non-normally distributed interval data and ordinal data	
	d	r (can be converted from d)	ω (or phi (Φ)), alternatively a version of r[1]	ηp^2 (partial eta squared)	W (Kendall's)	ηp^2 (partial eta squared)
Small	0.20	0.10	0.10	0.01	0.20	0.01
Medium	0.50	0.30	0.30	0.06	0.40	0.06
Large	0.80	0.50	0.50	0.14	0.60	0.14

Table 6.11. Commonly used effect sizes for reporting alongside p-values.

Name	Control	Name	Intervention A	Name	Intervention B
Bradford Baines	152	Melanie Dunn	156	Clorinda Austin	174
Rutha Cave	166	Millicent Imhoff	152	Porsche Bischoff	142
Sheron Aikin	138	Rosalina Derrow	196	Francesco Hayhurst	210
Maggie Kauppi	128	Yael Niccum	128	Analisa Linney	144
Elin Faddis	102	Harris Bogen	134	Laura Oldenburg	158
Maryjane Cypher	144	Elwanda Mang	166	Mary Ward	158

Table 6.12. Data from a between-participant post-test only design with three levels to the independent variable.

---

1 Different commentators have different views about which form of this statistic should be reported. Check the requirements of any publication you are writing for.

Name	Order in which the levels of the independent variable were experienced	Control	Intervention A	Intervention B
Suk Klann	Control → Intervention A → Intervention B	22.8	32.4	30.8
Veronique Ayers	Control → Intervention A → Intervention B	22.8	24.4	24.4
Diann Rizzi	Intervention A → Intervention B → Control	22.8	21.2	29.2
Alysa Bowyer	Intervention A → Intervention B → Control	32	32.8	32
German Sarris	Intervention B → Control → Intervention A	26	30.8	28.4
Noreen Eberle	Intervention B → Control → Intervention A	27.6	24.4	31.2

Table 6.13. Data from a within-participant (counterbalanced) post-test only design with three levels to the independent variable.

Family-wise error – how it can affect your results and one way to deal with it

If your study has more than two levels to the independent variable, you have introduced the probability that the results may be different just because there is a third element. This is known as family-wise error and it becomes a greater problem the more levels you have to your independent variable, or if you have multiple dependent variables that are all contributing to the same concept (e.g. scales in a personality test). Again, you will need to look at your software manual for how to deal with the different scenarios, but just so you understand the core concepts, we are going to run through the standard way to deal with this problem when you are working with three columns of data.

We have already mentioned a test called ANOVA. In fact, there are a number of different forms of ANOVA. The important thing, in terms of the issue we have just noted, is that they can all look at several columns of data at once. Furthermore, just are there are different types of inferential tests suitable for different situations when you have two levels to the independent variable, so there are different tests to use when you have three levels. The ones you will want to know about, and which you can use to analyse the designs we have discussed, are as follows:

- ANOVA – used for between-participant designs with normally distributed interval data and equal variance (with a few more subtle assumptions needing to be met).

- The Kruskal–Wallis test – the non-parametric alternative to ANOVA which does not mind what distribution you have and is the right test for ordinal data.

- Repeated measures ANOVA – the within-participant equivalent of ANOVA. In addition to the types of assumption you need to meet to use ANOVA, this test requires an assumption called sphericity to be met.

- The Friedman test – the non-parametric alternative to repeated measures ANOVA.

The way you use these tests is shown below (with the concept illustrated in Figure 6.9).

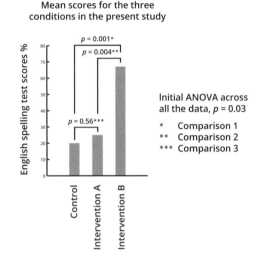

Figure 6.9. Multiple tests on data from a study with three levels to the independent variable.

Step 1

Perform an initial ANOVA across all the levels of the independent variable to determine if the overall change is significant. This is always a two-tailed test because, at this point, your hypothesis is simply that the things you are testing are different (a non-directional hypothesis).

Step 2

If the initial ANOVA result is significant then you conclude that any change is unlikely to be the result of family-wise error.

Step 3

Follow up by doing separate tests comparing two levels of the independent variable at a time (this is called doing contrasts or comparisons). These can be planned or post-hoc. Planned means that you decided to do these right from the start, and post-hoc means you are being more exploratory. Your software will use a slightly different test for each of these options and may have a number of variations you can choose from. The approach is more straightforward with non-parametric tests as you just follow the initial non-parametric version of ANOVA with the test you would usually use for two columns of data (e.g. the Mann–Whitney U test or the Wilcoxon signed-rank test).

Step 4

The usual guidance is to set a more stringent threshold that needs to be crossed for a finding to be considered significant. You do this with a Bonferroni adjustment. This means that you divide your threshold (or alpha) by the number of levels to your independent variable and thus the number of comparisons you will have to do. In this way, if you had planned to use a threshold of $\alpha = 0.05$ as your cut-off point, you adjust this to $0.05 / 3$ – a new threshold of $\alpha = 0.0167$. Practically, this means that studies with more than two levels to their independent variable need larger sample sizes to detect similar effects to studies with just two levels.

In the case of the inferential testing illustrated in Figure 6.9, we would conclude that the overall change was unlikely to be the result of family wise error ($p = 0.03$). With the threshold for significance set at $\alpha = 0.0167$ for the comparisons (i.e. $p < 0.0167$ is significant), we could interpret the result as follows:

- Intervention B improved spelling compared to both the control ($p = 0.001$) and intervention A ($p = 0.004$).

- Intervention A was equal to the approach used in the control ($p = 0.56$).

- **Brain Box 6.4. Example of results from one teacher-led study that had three levels to the independent variable and a pre- and post-test**

  This is an example of the style of reporting two teachers used for their findings from a within-participant design with three levels to the independent variable.[2]

---

2   Thanks to Rob Wilson and Gavin Jones for permission to include this data. The full report for this study can be found in Churches and McAleavy, *Evidence That Counts*.

Gain scores were analysed using the pre- and post-test data in Figure 6.10.

A Friedman test showed a significant difference across all conditions ($p < 0.001$). Separate Wilcoxon signed-rank tests were used to compare the three conditions with one another. Because the analysis used multiple tests, a more stringent significance level (Bonferroni adjustment) was set (0.0167). Separate comparisons showed that collaborative learning was significantly better than ordinary practice ($p < 0.001$), and collaborative learning with a template was significantly better than both these conditions ($p < 0.001$ and $p < 0.001$, respectively).

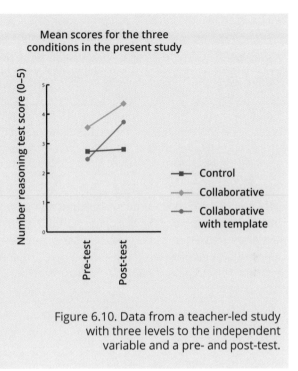

Figure 6.10. Data from a teacher-led study with three levels to the independent variable and a pre- and post-test.

Outliers – what are they, and what is the convention for dealing with them?

Outliers are another thing that you need to be aware of when analysing your data. An outlier is an observation (or score) within the data that sits at a distant point from other observations – in that it is beyond the distribution that might be expected. The main issue with outliers is that even a single one can cause your distribution to not be normally distributed. It could also result in the mean being unrepresentative.

A number of things can cause outliers. Typically, they may arise from:

- Data error – people make mistakes, especially when entering lots of numbers in a column.
- Deliberate or accidental misreporting by a participant for a whole host of reasons (which could include embarrassment or just not understanding the question).
- Sampling error – in other words, you have someone in your sample who is simply not representative of the population.

- Not maintaining your research protocol and not keeping it consistent – a sudden deviation from the procedures being used in your experiment.

- Outliers may also be a true representation of the thing you are researching.

Contrary to popular belief, outliers can affect the results of both parametric and non-parametric analyses. It is essential to identify if you have any outliers and decide what to do about them. You may need to consider removing them. If you do, you must reveal you did this in your reporting and justify their removal.

Inevitably, the idea of removing a participant, or participants, from your data after the treatment period is over has provoked much debate. The basic rule of thumb is that you should not remove an outlier just because it is an extreme score; you should only do so if you can be clear that it was caused by something exceptional – such as the definite mis-completion of a questionnaire or a traceable error.

All good statistical software has a function that allows you to identify outliers. You can also find free-to-use software online. Typically, outliers will be shown on a box plot with numbers indicating which data point (participant score) is the outlier, so you can identify them (see Figure 6.11).

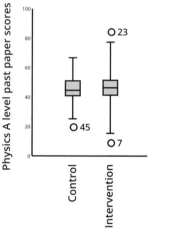

Box plot (with outliers) for the control and intervention groups

Figure 6.11. The typical way a number of software packages indicate outliers within a box plot.

Test yourself 6

Question 1

What are assumptions, and why are they important?

Question 2

Assuming the data was not normally distributed, identify the test you might use to analyse the following two studies:

A between-participant design was used with two levels to the independent variable. The control condition consisted of continuing with current maths practice in the teaching of coordinates. The intervention consisted of carefully planned active learning tasks and group work. After the treatment period (three weeks) both the control and intervention were given the same 20-question test and an average score was calculated for each child.

A within-participant design was used. Children were randomly allocated to the order in which they experienced two forms of marking feedback: the school's normal practice of giving a comment and a grade (control condition), and the same feedback but with the teacher colour coding aspects of their marking according to levels of importance (intervention). Essay writing was then assessed by a single-blind tester who used a GCSE mark scheme to produce an overall writing score.

Question 3

When would it be considered wrong to remove an outlier before conducting your analysis?

What next?

Now that you have learned about the principles of inferential testing, in the final chapter you will find out how to interpret your findings and disseminate them.

Chapter 7

Interpreting your findings and writing up your research

By the end of this chapter, you will know about:

- Interpreting your results, including dealing with non-significant findings.
- Reporting your findings in a conference poster.
- How you would approach writing up your results for a journal or preparing a talk.

Approaches to reporting your results

Unlike other styles of research, when it comes to experimental research people will expect you to write it up in a standard format that deviates little across different scientific fields. This chapter will explain how to write up your results in a conference poster style and then extend this to include journal article writing.

Conference style posters

Creating a conference poster is a great way to disseminate your research findings and explain them in an easy-to-digest way. You can also include photographs and other information in a poster. At an academic conference, posters are usually in an A1 or A2 size format and authors stand next to them so people can ask questions about the study.[1]

Being able to create a great poster is also a skill in its own right. More than that, having drafted a conference poster that is clear and concise, you will more easily be able to expand the text you have created to develop a longer journal article or even extend it to write a thesis for a qualification.

The structure of a typical reduced format conference poster is given in Figure 7.1. Using this reduced structure, you can quite successfully (if you write succinctly) communicate the main points within an A3 format.

Learning Zone 7.1. Finding conference poster designs online

The format we have suggested in Figure 7.1 works well for teacher-led experimental research projects, but is not the only format you could use. Type 'conference posters' into your search engine, select 'images' and take a look at a range of research posters that have applied a scientific method so you can get some ideas for layout.

Research reports in an academic journal

The summary conference poster format we have suggested is a reduced version of what has become a fairly standard format for the writing up of scientific papers in academic journals. The idea behind this relates to the central importance of replication within scientific method and it has an interesting historical basis (see Brain Box 7.1). The structure evolved from the practice of sharing the 'journal' in which you had recorded your experiment with others, so that they could repeat your exact steps. In this way, you would find out whether your results could be replicated and, if so, how frequently. From the perspective of replication, the key things that people need to know are:

- What the different conditions were.
- What type of test or measurement you used.
- What design you used (diagrams can be really helpful here).
- Who the participants were.

---

1   There are 12 examples of teacher-led experimental research presented in a conference poster style in Churches and McAleavy, *Evidence That Counts*, which is available online at: https://www.educationdevelopmenttrust.com.

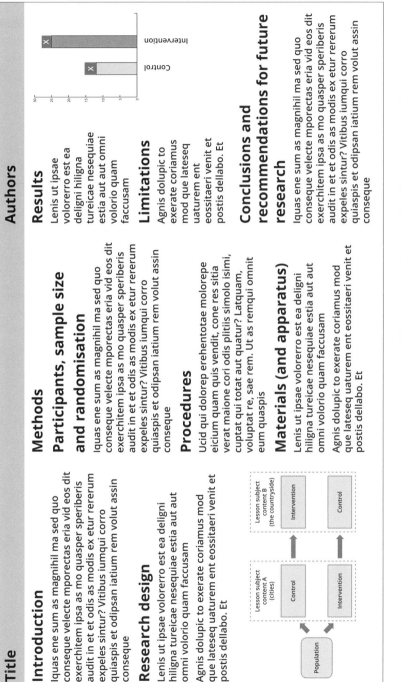

Figure 7.1. Possible structure for a teacher-led experimental research poster.

- What process you went through.
- What materials and apparatus (physical resources) were used in the experiment.

These pieces of information form the central body of a scientific journal article. Around these, the researcher begins by introducing the research and exploring the existing evidence from the literature and rationale for the research.

At the end of the article the results are presented (i.e. descriptive statistics, inferential tests used, effect sizes). The researcher then discusses what they think these results show, describing the effects, changes and patterns found and linking this to other research. Finally, conclusions are drawn, more speculative discussions take place, limitations in the research design and process are exposed honestly and some recommendations for future research stated.

Brain Box 7.1. Scientific journal articles – from secret to public

By the start of the 17th century, most researchers shared their research, although this was done mostly by letter writing and the exchange of correspondence. This all changed around 1660 when some cutting edge scientists, including Robert Boyle, Robert Hooke and Isaac Newton, set up secret meetings of a group they called 'the Invisible College'. This group grew and eventually evolved into the Royal Society. The format they adopted for sharing their experiments and findings was called a journal, which at that point included just one experiment in each publication. In 1665, what came to be called the *Philosophical Transactions* was established as the first scientific journal.

The process of sharing information in this way, in a clear, transparent and replicable form, transformed science and meant that knowledge could be quickly developed and shared. Most recognised journals include what is called peer review, a process whereby other people with knowledge of a similar area critique and give improvement feedback to the authors of a piece of research before it is published.

What to include in your write-up

Depending on the format of your write-up, the sections will contain either more or less detail – a journal article, for example, would require much more detail and more subsections than a conference poster. However, the content is usually organised within the following sections in the following order, although different journals will have different house style requirements.

Abstract

A short summary of the research and its findings (usually about 200–300 words).

Introduction

The introduction includes the background to the research and its rationale (in a formal journal article this would include a literature review), often ending with the aims and experimental hypothesis.

Methods

This section includes a number of subsections:

1   *Participants*: A description of the participants and how they were chosen. It is in this section that you need to specify how many participants you used, who they were and other information about them. It is pretty standard to include, as a minimum, the percentage of males and females and their ages, but other information may also be relevant. You would also explain any power analysis you did prior to the research to see how many participants you thought you might need to use and describe the randomisation process.

2   *Research design*: A section explaining the design of the study and detailing the different conditions and dependent variables. Note that so far we have tended to use the term 'condition', but in some cases you will see the levels of the independent variables described as 'groups'. People often ask us when they should use the different words. It's simple really: use group when you are referring to the people who experienced the condition, and condition when you are referring to the things they were exposed to. Thus, you might say: 'When the intervention group were exposed to the experimental condition it was noticeable that boys appeared to underperform compared to girls.' One obvious point to remember is that if your design is a within-participant design then all the children will have done both the control and intervention, so it would be very confusing to refer to a control group or intervention group in this case. Linguistically, you are left with only one option which is to talk about the 'control condition' and 'experimental condition' (or intervention) that the whole participant group experienced.

3   *Procedures*: An outline of the procedures used should include the specific pedagogy you applied and also a description of the processes you undertook. You may also need to mention how you managed the research – for example, if you gave the teachers any training and how they were briefed. This is a good place to mention what you did to reduce the impact of any extraneous variables and remove any confounding variables.

4   *Materials*: An outline of the materials and other physical resources you used. This final part of the methods section is also the place to describe the numerical measures that were applied and any information you have about their validity and reliability. It is also where, in a school context, you might mention room layout for the conditions and any teacher resources you think it might be important for someone replicating your study to know about.

5   *Data analysis:* An explanation of the statistical analysis used.

Results

In this section, you state the results without discussing them. It is good practice to repeat what test you used, the effect size and the level of significance attained. You will also include any relevant descriptive data (such as means and standard deviation, as appropriate). This section would normally contain figures or tables to summarise your data and make it easier to understand.

Discussion

In this section, you discuss what you think the results mean. This section may be merged with the conclusion. As well as reporting your findings you need to describe the limitations of your work. This is the part of the report where you challenge yourself for not having done the impossible (creating the perfect research design)! This gives you the opportunity to demonstrate your ability to recognise the limitations of your study. In the light of your findings and the limitations, you then make recommendations for future research. A good example of this would be if you found a moderate effect size (such as $d = 0.40$) but your inferential testing on this effect did not reach a level of probability that could be considered significant ($p = 0.07$). Such a situation will be partly the result of the sample size having been too small. As we saw in Chapter 5, you need 78 participants in the control and 78 in the intervention in a between-participant design for a $d = 0.40$ effect size to be significant (one-tailed) at $p < 0.05$. In this case, your recommendation would be for a larger replication.

Conclusion

The conclusion is where you can state what you think you found overall in light of everything you have said. It may also be appropriate, depending on the study, to be more speculative about the implications of the findings based on your reading of the literature and suggest a new theory.

References

A list of the publications that you have cited in your report.

Writing research papers is an art but one of the things that really helps is reading other people's research. This will support you to develop an appropriate style of writing and to write more succinctly.

Learning Zone 7.2. Challenge your design and results

If you are reading this and are about to write a limitations section, take a look back at the advantages and disadvantages of the different designs we discussed in Chapter 3 and the section on extraneous and confounding variables in Chapter 2, and reflect on your design and results. Identify the key limitations that remain in your study and state them. Then think about what recommendations you will make for future research at the end of your report.

Learning Zone 7.3. Read an online article

There are many free-to-download journal articles online. If you go to Google Scholar (scholar. google.com) and search for 'experiment journal' and then click on any PDFs that you find, you will soon find some examples. You can also sign up to various online journals, such as *The Lancet*.

Some of the papers you find will be more detailed statistically than the approaches we have introduced you to here, but the more articles you look at, the more you will be able to make sense of the approaches and style of writing used. In any case, even if you are not be looking to produce a journal article, reading other people's research will help you to develop your writing technique.

If you want to look at some reports that are halfway between a conference poster and a formal journal article – a more teacher-friendly approach, perhaps – you may want to look at the following examples, both of which can be found on the Education Development Trust website:

Richard Churches and James Gibbs, *Mindfulness: A Small-Scale Study of the Effects of Teacher Work-Related Stress on the Structure of Consciousness, and the Use of Mindfulness In Its Management* (Reading: CfBT Education Trust, 2013).

Richard Churches and Fiona Allan, *Raising Maths Attainment Through Enhanced Pedagogy and Communication: Results from a 'Teacher-Level' Randomised Controlled Trial* (Reading: CfBT Education Trust, 2013).

Now we have gone through the main things to include in your write-up, we are going to look in depth at the results section because this is the part of the reporting that includes the most technical and specific language. We are going to do this with some straightforward short examples in the style that you might use in a summary conference poster. We will then go on to explain the more extended forms of statistics that you might need to use if you were to publish in a journal. Finally, we will consider a few sticking points that make reporting results tricky!

Results section

If you have plenty of space it is normal to report your descriptive statistics first (e.g. means and standard deviations if your data is normally distributed, and median and range if your data is not normally distributed) and then go on to report your inferential statistics and effect size (see Brain Box 7.2). However, it is also possible to amalgamate these into a single piece of reporting.

Below you can find four examples of how you might write up your findings. The first three show how you might write up your results if the finding was significant and the final one if it was not.

Example 1 – Reporting descriptive statistics first, then inferential testing and effect size for parametric data (between-participant two conditions)

Children in the intervention appeared to score higher on the maths test than those in the control condition (see Table 7.1).

An independent samples *t*-test indicated a significant difference between the intervention and control ($p = 0.01$ (one-tailed)), with a medium effect size ($d = 0.45$).

Condition	Maths score	
	Mean	SD
Control	25.5	17.3
Intervention	34.2	21.1

Table 7.1. Mean score and standard deviation (SD) for the control and intervention.

Example 2 – Reporting descriptive statistics and inferential testing at the same time for parametric data (within-participant two conditions)

A paired sample t-test indicated a significant ($p = 0.03$) difference between the intervention (mean = 45.5, SD = 18.3) and control (mean = 37.2, SD = 27) indicating that the intervention has a moderate effect on pupils' attainment ($d = 0.36$).

Example 3 – Reporting descriptive and inferential testing at the same time for non-parametric data (between-participant two conditions)

A Mann–Whitney U test indicated a significant decrease ($p = 0.02$) in the attainment of the intervention group (median = 40.5, range = 25) compared to the control group (median = 35, range = 26), with a small negative effect on attainment ($r = -0.10$).

Notice, as explained in Chapters 5 and 6, how we have used different tests for different types of design and (as discussed above) reported the mean and standard deviation for normally distributed data but the median and range for data that was not normally distributed.

Of course, in the real world you might replace the word 'intervention' with, for example, the name of the pedagogy you used and 'control' with something like 'normal practice' in order to make the results easier to understand.

In the next example, a non-significant effect has been reported.

Example 4 – Reporting descriptive and inferential testing at the same time for non-parametric data (between-participant pre- and post-test design where gain scores have been used)

Gain scores were first calculated from pre- and post-test scores. A Mann–Whitney U test indicated no difference ($p = 0.54$) between the control (median = 8.5, range = 5) and intervention (median = 8.6, range = 4.2), the effect size was medium ($r = 0.32$).

One point to make here is that if you have non-significance, the robust position is that there is no difference and therefore no actual effect size has been detected, so many people would argue you should not report the effect size at all where the result is non-significant. However, this depends on the context of your experiment and personal point of view. Either way, if your result is non-significant you will not be concluding that one condition was different to another.

Brain Box 7.2. Reporting inferential statistics more formally

As we explained in Chapters 5, different tests have different test statistics. It is customary in journals to report the test statistic along with either the degrees of freedom or sample size and an effect size statistic, with different effect size statistics used with different inferential statistics. Table 7.2 provides examples of the sort of requirements that might be expected in a journal or in postgraduate level research projects.

Test	Test statistic	Degrees of freedom	Effect size
Independent samples *t*-test	t	Report just the denominator in brackets after t	d
Paired sample *t*-test	t	Report just denominator in brackets after t	dz (or d)
Mann–Whitney *U* test	U if the sample size is small, but Z if it is reasonably large (> 40 is what most people recommend for U)	Report sample size instead	r
Wilcoxon signed-rank test	Z	Report sample size instead	r
Chi-squared test of independence	χ^2 (chi-squared)	Report sample size instead	ω (or phi (Φ), alternatively a version of r that produces the same value)[2]
ANOVA and ANCOVA	F	Report df with numerator and denominator in brackets after For example: $F(1, 345) = 4.50$	ηp^2 (partial eta squared)

2 Different commentators have different views about which form of this statistic should be reported. Check the requirements of any publication you are writing for.

Test	Test statistic	Degrees of freedom	Effect size
Kruskal–Wallis test	χ^2 (chi-squared)	Report sample size instead	ω (or phi (Φ), alternatively Rosenthal's r which produces the same value)
Friedman's ANOVA	χ^2 (chi-squared)	Report sample size instead	Kendall's W
Repeated measures ANOVA	F	The same as ANOVA unless you violate an assumption known as sphericity, in which case your degrees of freedom will end up decimal not integer (whole number)	ηp^2 (partial eta squared)

Table 7.2. Conventions for reporting test statistics and degrees of freedom in the tests we have covered (in the order we covered them).

To see the interpretations you can apply to the different effect sizes mentioned above, see Table 6.11 in Chapter 6.

These statistics are usually reported together at the same time as your p-value and using a similar structure to the examples below.

A paired sample t-test indicated a significant improvement in attainment in response to group work (mean = 27.01, SD = 7.19) compared to normal practice (mean = 24.1, SD = 7.68), $t(734) = 4.31$, $p < 0.0001$, $dz = 0.43$.

A Mann–Whitney U test showed that boys' learning (median = 5, range = 3) improved significantly compared to girls' (median = 4, range = 4), $U(35) = 67.5$, $p = 0.034$, $r = 0.38$.

What's the point of that, we hear you say, as surely the only useful things are the effect size and the p-value? Although this is true from the point of view of interpreting your findings, reporting the test statistic and degrees of freedom (or the sample size) can enable someone else to look up your results in a critical table and make sure that your significance level is in the right ballpark.

How many decimal places to go to when writing up

One thing you may be wondering as you read this is why some values are given as whole numbers and others are given to three or four decimal places. There is no hard and fast rule about this. This said, here are some guidelines to get you started.

Numbers with a value greater than 100 are usually reported to the nearest whole number (e.g. mean = 7325). Numbers between 10 and 100 are reported to one decimal place (e.g. mean = 39.2). For numbers between 0.10 and 10, two decimal places are reported (e.g. mean = 4.52, SD = 0.98). Numbers that have a value less than 0.10 should be reported to three decimal places (e.g. 0.003). However, you should use as many digits as necessary where numbers are close to zero (e.g. mean = 0.016, SEM = 0.0002). In relation to p-values, it is common these days to use exact numbers (to three decimal places), with the exception of occasions where software has reported 0.000, which is usually reported as $p < 0.001$. Occasionally, when it is not possible to report the exact p-value, the convention of < (less than) or > (more than) the level of alpha you set can be adopted (e.g. $p < 0.05$ or $p > 0.05$).

Keeping graphs simple

Using graphs can also be helpful as long as you don't make them too complicated. It is very tempting to go overboard, especially now that Excel enables you to do all sorts of things with the design. Remember that your main aim should be to communicate clearly what you have found. Stick to simple structures like the examples in Figure 7.2.

If you feel that it helps, you can also add what are called 'whiskers' to indicate elements like the confidence interval or standard error of the mean (which we covered in Chapter 5).

Confidence intervals

Confidence intervals are a very useful measure to report in your write-up. These estimate the range in which the mean is likely to fall in a certain number of repeated experiments. Thus, they can be seen as a measure of generalisability. You would not, however, normally report confidence intervals *instead* of the significance level but in addition

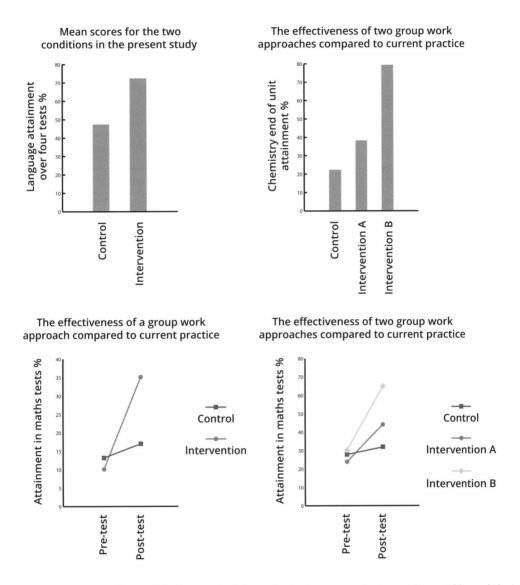

Figure 7.2. Easy-to-build graphs that communicate results quickly and their uses. Top left: two levels to the IV and a post-test only. Top right: three levels to the IV and a post-test only. Bottom left: two levels to the IV, pre- and post-test design. Bottom right: three levels to the IV, pre- and post-test design.

to significance and effect size. Finding that your results might be likely to generalise adds weight to your ability to make a claim regarding the validity of your study.

Here is how confidence intervals work and how to interpret them. You can calculate confidence intervals in Excel, in most statistics packages and in online tests. The results from doing this will be presented in the format demonstrated in Table 7.3 (or similar).

Condition	Mean score	Standard deviation	Lower bound	Upper bound
Control	56.1	40.9	47.7	79.7
Intervention	87.5	35.2	64.3	94.3

Table 7.3. Means, standard deviation and confidence intervals from a two-condition study.

Lower bound means the bottom of the likely range of means in a certain number of replications. Upper bound means the upper end of the range. The usual level set for confidence intervals is 95%. In other words, the lower and upper bound ranges indicate where your mean is likely to fall in 95 out of 100 repeated studies. However, this can't replace replication!

By transferring these ranges onto a graph with whiskers, you end up with something like the graphs in Figure 7.3. If the range bars do not overlap then you can be confident that in 95% of repeated studies a similar result might be found.

As the calculation of confidence intervals, like significance, includes your sample size, the larger your sample, the more likely you are to find a gap between the ranges.

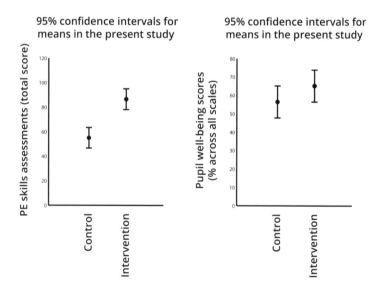

Figure 7.3. The left-hand graph shows 95% confidence intervals in a two-condition study which is likely to be replicable. The right-hand graph shows 95% confidence intervals in a two-condition study which is not likely to replicate.

Sticking point 1

One issue that can make reporting results tricky is telling the difference between having identified an alternative treatment and identifying something that does not work. The classic example of this, and where it is easy to interpret things incorrectly, is with regard to studies where the control condition is not 'doing nothing' (a negative control) but rather involves 'doing something' (a positive control).

Take the following two examples where we will interpret the same data but in the context of two different experiments. Firstly, imagine we found that there was no difference between our control condition and our experimental condition, with the inferential test showing $p = 0.87$ (two-tailed) and the effect size $r = 0.003$ (a very small effect) (see Figure 7.4).

Imagine that in the first experiment our research design involved children in their summer holiday *not* attending a catch-up summer school (the control) compared to a group that *did* attend a catch-up summer school (the intervention). In this case, our conclusions might be that the summer school makes no difference and that it is not worth attending or running.

Now, imagine that we had exactly the same data but had compared normal best practice in the classroom (as the control) with a new teaching approach (the intervention). In this case, we would be concluding that the new approach is equal to existing practice and therefore an alternative treatment.

In the case of a pre- and post-test design, no difference would be illustrated in a graph by the existence of equal or similar slopes (see Figure 7.5). However, the same principle would apply.

Although it is early days for experimental research in schools, our experience of about 80 teacher-led studies suggests that teacher-led research is likely to find about 40% of

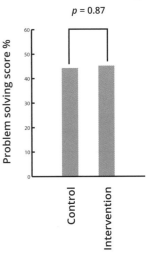

Mean attainment for the control and intervention group

Figure 7.4. Example data in which there is no difference between the control and the intervention.

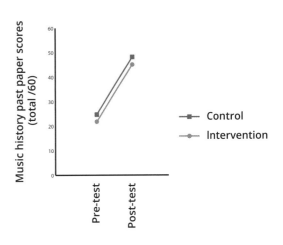

Mean pre- and post-test scores for the control and intervention

Figure 7.5. Example data from a pre- and post-test design showing no difference between control and intervention.

treatments to be equal to existing practice and thus an alternative treatment. Equally, 40–50% of practice seems to be improved through innovation. Lastly, and very occasionally, a small proportion of teachers detect negative effects on attainment compared to normal practice.

Finding no difference between the control condition and the intervention when the control is 'existing best practice' has to be a good thing for the teaching profession, because every alternative treatment identified that is equal to another approach expands the range of strategies that teachers can use without fear of doing any harm. In the same way, a doctor often has a range of different pharmaceuticals that could be prescribed for a particular patient but he/she is able to make a professional choice about what would be best in this situation.

Sticking point 2

Another point that can be hard to get your head around occurs when you have a moderate or large effect but a non-significant result. Remember that your p-value is a function of (i.e. is made up of) effect size calculations *plus* sample size, whereas an effect size calculation does not depend on the volume of data. Therefore, it is possible to have a large effect that is not significant, which is caused by your sample size being too small.

If you find a moderate or large effect that is not significant, an appropriate interpretation would be that, although the results show no difference, the study can be seen as providing preliminary evidence for an effect and make the case for a larger replication – particularly if the results were close to significance (or 'approached significance').

Sticking point 3

The final sticking point is choosing a title based on your results. If you find a significant result, choosing a title is easy as you can just use your experimental hypothesis (if you wrote it in the present tense). For example:

> Three lessons of group work improves column addition problem-solving with Year 6 rural primary school pupils.

If your results are non-significant you will have to decide on a title that reflects the context and research design you used. It might be that you just decide to state your null hypothesis. For example:

> Three lessons of group work does not improve column addition problem-solving with Year 6 rural primary school pupils.

However, if you ended up with one of the interpretations we talked about earlier, such as having identified an alternative treatment, you might decide on something like this:

Evidence that illustrates an alternative approach to column addition problem-solving in a Year 6 primary school lesson.

Or maybe:

Alternative approaches to column addition problem-solving in a rural primary school.

Another possibility that might arise is when you have a reasonable effect size that is not significant. In this case, with a small sample size your study should probably be classed as a pilot study:

Evidence from a small-scale pilot study regarding the effectiveness of group work in primary school column addition problem-solving.

Another option, depending on the strength of the effect, could be to use the word 'preliminary':

Preliminary evidence for the effectiveness of group work in improving column addition problem-solving.

Whatever title you choose, it is a good idea to select something which immediately communicates your findings and which is not too cryptic.

Brain box 7.3. A teacher example of how descriptive statistics, inferential testing and effect size all come together when interpreting your results

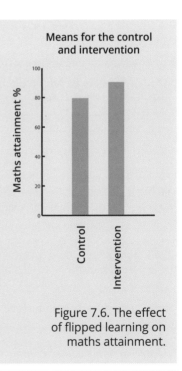

Means for the control and intervention

Figure 7.6. The effect of flipped learning on maths attainment.

Two teachers (Matthew Maughan and David Ashton) carried out a piece of research across schools in Wales.[3] They looked at whether flipped learning would improve attainment in a maths lesson compared to an identical lesson without flipped learning. As they had a within-participant design and interval data, but found that their data was not normally distributed, they used the Wilcoxon signed-rank test to compare the attainment of the children when they were in the flipped learning lessons to the non-flipped lessons.

Reading the one-tailed result (because they had a one-tailed hypothesis), the outcome of doing this showed that there was a statistically significant difference for the flipped learning ($p = 0.002$). The result was considered significant, in this

---

3   Thanks to Matthew Maughan and David Ashton for letting us quote their study. The full report can be found in Churches and McAleavy, *Evidence That Counts*.

case, because the *p*-value was less than $p = 0.05$ (the usual threshold for significance and the one they had adopted for the study). Their *p*-value ($p = 0.002$), although it told them that the change was significant, did not tell them in which direction the change had taken place (i.e. whether flipped learning improved attainment or not compared to the non-flipped learning lesson). To figure this out, they had to look back at their descriptive data and the median scores (because they had used a non-parametric test).

Looking at this data, it was clear that the flipped learning lesson resulted in higher attainment than the non-flipped learning. They then also calculated and reported the effect size and found that this was $r = 0.26$. This told them the strength of the change (a medium effect).

They were then able to write up the results:

> A Wilcoxon signed-rank test indicated a significant ($p = 0.002$) improvement in attainment for pupils who were exposed to the flipped learning method (mdn[4] = 100), compared to the control (mdn = 90). A medium effect size ($r = 0.26$).

Referencing in your write-up

Irrespective of whether you are producing a conference poster or research report, you will need to provide references for any research to which you have referred. For research reports, the journal will normally have quite clear guidelines on what to do and specify a certain style (see Learning Zone 7.4). For conference posters, however, there is less likely to be guidance provided on exactly what to do but you will still be expected to use a recognised style of referencing (e.g. the Harvard referencing system). However, the critical thing is this: whatever style you use, you must be consistent.

Referencing not only includes providing a list of references at the end of your document, but also making it clear which ideas are attributed to the different sources throughout the text. You do this using an 'in-text citation'. The simplest way to do this is to give the author(s) and year in brackets after the idea that you are referring to – for example:

> As many writers note, when analysing your data it is essential to use the right statistical test to assess whether your findings are significant or not (Churches and Dommett, 2016; Field, 2013).

Direct quotations should include the page reference and you should indicate clearly that this is a quotation:

> 'We delivered workshops on neuroscience emphasising brain plasticity to 11–12 year old pupils to encourage belief in incremental intelligence … Neuroscience training increased belief

---

4   'Mdn' is the usual abbreviation for median.

in incremental intelligence over the 20 months but had no specific effects on other motivational measures or maths performance.' (Dommett et al., 2013: 122)

There are two important things to notice about the quotation above. It is acceptable to miss bits out of a long quotation by indicating this with an ellipsis, but you should not do this at the expense of the original meaning. Also, notice the use of 'et al.' (short for the Latin *et alia*, meaning 'and others'). Often, if a publication has more than three authors, house styles will ask you to mention only the lead author name followed by 'et al.' This has been included above because there were four authors for this publication (Eleanor Dommett, Ian Devonshire, Emma Sewter and Susan Greenfield).

You would then include the full reference for these publications within a section at the end of your report called 'references' – for example, using the Harvard referencing system:

Churches, R. and Dommett, E. (2016). *Teacher-Led Research: Designing and Implementing Randomised Controlled Trials and Other Forms of Experimental Research* (Carmarthen: Crown House Publishing).

Dommett, E., Devonshire, I. M., Sewter, E. and Greenfield, S. A. (2013). 'The impact of participation in a neuroscience course on motivational measures and academic performance', *Trends in Neuroscience and Education* 2(3–4): 122–138.

Field, A. (2013). *Discovering Statistics Using IBM SPSS Statistics*, 4th edn (London: SAGE).

Notice the difference between a book reference and a journal article. The journal article also includes details of the volume and issue where the journal article can be found – in this case '2(3–4)'. It also includes the page span within the journal (as a journal will usually contain multiple articles).

Information like this is easy to find because it will appear on the journal article itself. If you cite an article that is available online, or a piece of material that is only online (such as conference slides), it is good practice to give the date you accessed the publication (as below), perhaps adding a DOI number. This can help people to search for the material you have cited.

Churches, R. (2015). 'The followership effect: charismatic oratory, hypnoidal and altered states of consciousness' (conference oral presentation slides), Fifth Annual Postgraduate Research Conference, University of Surrey, 25 April. Available at: http://www.researchgate.net/publication/274833267_The_Followership_Effect_Charismatic_Oratory_Hypnoidal_and_Altered_States_of_Consciousness (accessed 3 June 2015). DOI: 10.13140/RG.2.1.4760.5285

Learning Zone 7.4. Looking at referencing examples

Take several academic-style books off your bookshelf and take a few moments to thumb through them, noticing how the referencing has been done and what has been cited. Then turn to the references section at the end of the book and look at the different ways that books, journal articles and other materials have been referenced. Finally, compare the house style differences between the publications.

Test yourself 7

Question 1

Explain what is meant by a confidence interval.

Question 2

Write a results statement to describe the following, assuming a p-value of 0.003 and an effect size of $d = 0.52$:

Condition	Correct spellings	
	Mean	SD
Control	15	4
Intervention	23	5

Table 7.4. Hypothetical mean score and standard deviation (SD) for the control and intervention.

Concluding remarks

We began this book with the ambitious aim to encourage experimental research led by teachers themselves and to support a more diverse research style in the field of education. As you have worked your way through, you may have already started to think about and plan your own research. We hope that as you firm up your plans you will also reuse the Learning Zone boxes to produce a detailed, step-by-step approach to your study. Inevitably, this topic cannot be given an in-depth handling in a single book and we have skirted over some issues, particularly the full range of statistical approaches that are possible. However, we hope that, armed with this book and the further recommended reading we have touched on, you can start to create the firm scientific research that will provide evidence for future education strategies and teachers!

Remember that collecting qualitative data alongside your results from quantitative measures (a mixed method approach) can be a powerful way of enhancing and helping you to interpret your findings. You may also like to think about the possibilities of embedding your randomised controlled trials into a development cycle, integrating different approaches in order to draw on the strengths of different research methods (see Figure C.1).

In this example, teacher qualitative case study work has led the way in exploring classroom pedagogies that might be suitable for solving a school improvement issue. This initial work has then been used to define the protocols and an intervention that could be tested in a pilot experimental study. Once this has been completed, a larger collaborative randomised controlled trial has been designed and implemented. Finally, teacher action research is undertaken in order to explore the best ways to design and embed training approaches related to the intervention.

Finally, the types of statistics that you will learn to use as you develop your quantitative research skills can be just as powerful for understanding what is going on in your school in relation to general school data and are applicable to a wide range of school improvement questions. For example, you might want to test if this year's GCSE results really are significantly better than last year's or calculate the effect size for an approach that you are implementing for the first time.

To contact Richard please email rchurches@cfbt.com.

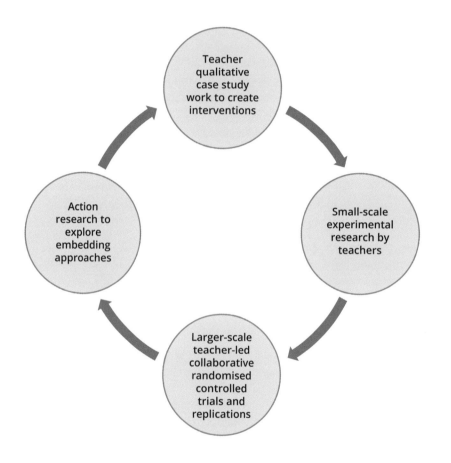

Figure C.1. An integrated mixed method approach.

Test yourself answers

Here you can find the answers to the self-assessment questions posed at the end of each of the chapters.

Test yourself 1

Answer 1

Findings in research are all related to the probability that the result may have happened by chance, so there is always the possibility we may be wrong. Replication helps to solve this problem because if the result is really true then we are likely to find it repeated more times than not.

Answer 2

This is an observational study because the researcher is not allocating the children to the conditions but taking measurements from those who already practise these behaviours.

Answer 3

You could have had any of the advantages or disadvantages listed in the section 'Types of experimental research'. For example, it is objective and quick to collect data but it cannot tell you about personal factors such as belief – and only you get out what you put in.

Test yourself 2

Answer 1

It is a two-tailed hypothesis because it states that there will be an effect but not the direction of the effect.

Answer 2

You could have suggested a number of options here – an obvious choice would be to have all girls (level 1), all boys (level 2) and a balance of both (level 3).

Answer 3

The reliability of your dependent variable refers to whether, if you were to repeat the test or questionnaire, it is likely to produce the same results for the same group of participants or different ones.

Test yourself 3

Answer 1

Individual differences are the differences that may be present between the participants in your study. They are a problem for between-participant designs because they could result in two different groups of people completing the two conditions of your study. If this is the case, it would be hard to ascertain whether any differences in the dependent variable are due to the independent variable rather than individual differences. This is not a problem for within-participant designs because the same people take part in both conditions.

Answer 2

Because the researcher only has a small group of pupils, a within-participant design is likely to be needed. The two conditions would be original warm-up exercises and modified warm-up exercises. The participants would need to be randomly allocated to the order of the conditions. The different warm-up exercises are unlikely to have a long lasting or irreversible effect so could be split across just two PE lessons.

Answer 3

It is necessary to counterbalance to avoid order effects – for example, practice effects or fatigue effects that would otherwise affect performance on a task.

Test yourself 4

Answer 1

Demand characteristics are subtle and not so subtle cues that can lead participants to become consciously or unconsciously aware of the purpose of an experiment, thereby making them behave differently, often tending towards behaving in a way they think the task demands.

Answer 2

A double-blind experiment prevents experimenter bias or participant effects impacting on the results because neither are aware of the condition of individual participants.

Answer 3

Chance bias may occur so that randomisation, rather than resulting in two similar groups, in fact results in a considerable imbalance with regard to participants' characteristics, which might end up affecting your results.

Test yourself 5

Answer 1

Exactly how you word this will vary but we think it should be something along the lines of: 'Introducing peer marking into maths classes increased the mean score from 64% to 69%. However, there was also an increase in the spread of the data, with a much greater standard deviation in the experimental condition.'

Answer 2

For a two-tailed hypothesis, a p-value of 0.02 would mean that there was a 2 in 100 probability that the result observed arose by chance. The normal alpha level set for two-tailed hypotheses is alpha $= 0.05$, therefore this would class as significance if the standard alpha was used.

Answer 3

Power analysis is the process of determining the sample size you will need in order to not miss a particular effect size that you have predicted may be there.

Test yourself 6

Answer 1

Assumptions are the rules that determine which inferential test is the right one for your research design, the type of data produced by the dependent variable you want to test and the distribution of the data.

Answer 2

The first example could be analysed with the Mann–Whitney U test, the second with the Wilcoxon signed-rank test.

Answer 3

You should not remove an outlier just because it is an outlier. Outliers should only be removed if you can explain them and their removal can be justified, so you can avoid being accused of manipulating the data.

Test yourself 7

Answer 1

A confidence interval is an estimate of whether the results would replicate a certain proportion of the time. As such, it represents a measure of generalisability. Usually the level is set at 95% and is expressed as a range within which, if a study were repeated 100 times, the mean would be likely to fall in 95% of those repetitions.

Answer 2

The exact wording may differ but similar information should be included: 'Children in the intervention (mean = 23) appeared to score higher on the spelling test than those in the control condition (mean = 15), with both groups having a similar standard deviation. The difference was shown to be significant ($p = 0.003$) and of moderate effect size ($d = 0.52$).'

Glossary

One of the challenges in learning to do this type of research is that often there are many alternative names for the different concepts and tests. We have therefore provided a glossary so you can see the relationship between the commonest variations in vocabulary that you will come across and the terminology that we have used in this book.

A

Alpha Alpha is the term used for the threshold of significance that you set at the beginning of your research project. This is never greater than 0.05 (a 5 in 100 probability that the result may have been arrived at by chance) but you can set a more stringent level such as 0.01 or 0.001.

B

Between-participant post-test design A study where you have assigned different people to different experiences (or conditions) within your research. For example, one group of people might experience the control condition while another group experience the intervention (or experimental condition). You measure the dependent variable only after they have experienced the condition. Also referred to as between-subject, independent measures or independent samples.

Between-participant pre- and post-test design A study where you have assigned different people to different experiences (or conditions) within your research. For example, one group of people might experience the control condition while another group experience the intervention (or experimental condition). You measure the dependent variable both before and after they have experienced the condition. The before tests allow you to check the groups for similarity. Also referred to as between-subject, independent measures or independent samples.

Bidirectional hypothesis (two-tailed) A hypothesis that does not specify the direction of the effect of the independent variable on the dependent variable.

Blind (or single-blind) experiment A piece of experimental or quasi-experimental research in which the participants do not know what condition they are in when they are experiencing it. For example, in a classroom-based within-participant design (although aware that there is research going on), the participants might not be aware of the shift in conditions or that the study is a randomised controlled trial.

C

Carry-over effects In a within-participant design, the ability of one condition of your independent variable to have effects that are sufficiently long lasting to impact on the condition participants would experience afterwards. In such a situation you would probably need to use a between-participant design instead.

Ceiling effect When a test does not have a high enough range to truly reflect attainment in the real world and therefore cuts off levels of high attainment that should be represented. See also **floor effect**.

Chance bias A problem that can occur when simple random allocation is used. It is perfectly possible to use simple randomisation but end up with an imbalance in the characteristics of your samples by chance. Processes like stratified randomisation and case-matching can reduce this problem.

Confidence interval An estimate of whether the results would replicate a certain proportion of the time. As such, it represents a measure of generalisability. Usually the level is set at 95% and expressed as a range within which, if a study were repeated

100 times, the mean would fall in 95% of those repetitions.

Confounding variable A variable other than the dependent variable that varies systematically with the manipulation of the independent variable. For example, if two different classrooms were used for the control (IV level 1) and intervention (IV level 2) but the intervention classroom had no natural lighting and very little space compared to the control classroom, resulting in lower attainment for this group.

Counterbalancing The practice of reversing the order of conditions for a proportion of the participants to avoid order effects.

D

Degrees of freedom (df) The number of values that are free to vary within the calculations that are performed by inferential tests. When reported in a journal article format, many tests will include two types of degrees of freedom.

Demand characteristics Subtle and not so subtle cues that can lead participants to become consciously or unconsciously aware of the purpose of an experiment, making them behave differently – often in a way which tends towards performing how they think the study requires them to perform.

Dependent variable (DV) The measure, or test, that varies according to your manipulation of the independent variable. For example, if your study looked at the effects of a creative writing week on children's writing skills, you might give them a short story to write as a test at the end of the week and mark it. The difference between the control (IV level 1) and intervention (IV level 2) on this test would be the dependent variable.

Descriptive statistics The type of statistics that just describe what is there (in contrast to inferential statistics). These include things like the mean, median, standard deviation, range, standard error of the mean and effect sizes of various sorts.

Directional hypothesis (one-tailed) A hypothesis that specifies the direction of the effect of the independent variable on the dependent variable.

Double-blind experiment A trial which adds another level of blindness to a single-blind trial by ensuring that the researcher is not aware of which condition participants are in. Further, the person managing the data will also be blind to who was in the control and intervention.

E

Effect size Ways of describing in a single number the strength of a phenomenon that has been observed. It is generally considered good practice to report the effect size as well as the level of significance (p). However, an effect can't really be claimed to exist if the p-value is not significant (i.e. it has not crossed the threshold set for the rejection of the null hypothesis). Common effect sizes include: d, r, ω and ηp^2. Each of these is suitable for use with a particular type of data and needs to be interpreted differently.

Experimental research Research in which the researcher assigns participants to conditions that have been designed by the researcher.

Experimenter effect Any change in your data that has been caused by the fact that you did the measurement in the first place. This can be your own biases which end up being transferred into the research design or your way of measuring the effects.

Experimental hypothesis The type of hypothesis which states that the independent variable will have an effect on the dependent variable.

Extraneous variable An external influence that has the potential to affect the result of your research, but which does not vary systematically with the manipulation of the independent variable.

F

Floor effect When a test does not have a low enough range to reflect true attainment and has therefore exaggerated the lowest levels of attainment. See also **ceiling effect**.

H

Hypothesis A statement of the answer to a research question that can be tested, proved or disproved. It is normal to have both a null hypothesis and an experimental hypothesis.

I

Independent variable (IV) The thing that you are manipulating in your experiment by creating different experiences for your participants. The different experiences (or conditions) are in turn called the levels of the independent variable. For example, a study that looked at peer reading might have two levels to the IV:

- IV level 1 (control) – Normal classroom practice
- IV level 2 (intervention) – Normal classroom practice with the addition of peer reading

Informed consent The formal written consent that must be given by participants in a research study prior to beginning data collection. All participants must be informed of the aims, risks and benefits of the research. This document is normally part of the information approved by an ethics committee.

Information sheet The information provided to participants to inform them about a study, including its aims and what it will involve. This document is normally part of the information approved by an ethics committee.

Inferential statistics Any statistical test which produces a p-value allowing the researcher to infer the extent to which their findings may have been the result of chance or not. The assessment of such probabilities is the basis of scientific method.

Interval data Data in which the difference between individual scores is known as well as what that difference means exactly. For example, measuring height in centimetres or the mean scores from a test paper in which there are a number of questions. Interval data is sometimes referred to as scale data.

L

Levels The different conditions of the independent variable.

M

Matched pairs design A research design in which participants have been paired (or case-matched) according to characteristics they share prior to allocation to a condition.

Mean The average value typically used to describe normally distributed data.

Median The average value typically used to describe data that is not normally distributed.

Meta-analysis The combination of quantitative data from a large number of studies. Just adding these up and averaging them is not enough, however, and there are sophisticated methods that should be used to conduct a meta-analysis. Such studies should not attempt to combine things from different domains; in the same way that it makes no sense to average bananas and umbrellas in the same sum (unless you want a bumbrella!).

Mundane realism The extent to which what happens in an experiment is similar to what would take place within the day-to-day experience of the participants.

N

Negative control The group in which no change is expected because they have not experienced anything.

Nominal data The type of numerical data that you could put into a pot and then count (e.g. the number of yes or no votes). It is also sometimes referred to as categorical data.

Non-parametric tests Inferential tests which are suitable for non-normally distributed interval data and data which breaks other assumptions of normality. These tests are also, by default, the test to use on ordinal data.

Normal distribution Data which, when put into a histogram, has the shape of a bell curve.

Null hypothesis The type of hypothesis which states that the independent variable will have no effect on the dependent variable.

O

Observational research Research where the researcher observes and makes measures from pre-existing groups or conditions rather than attempting to allocate to conditions, even though allocation is possible.

One-tailed hypothesis see **directional hypothesis**.

Order effects Effects that arise in your data purely because of the order in which participants experienced the conditions.

Ordinal data Data that involves some form of rank ordering. For example, where participants were rank ordered according to ability rather than given a specific mark based on a mark scheme of some sort. Ordinal data is also data which is constructed from subjective scales such as the Likert scale.

P

Parametric tests Types of inferential test suitable for use with normally distributed data.

Positive control The group which experience a condition that is known to have an effect but is not the experimental condition. For example, having a condition where current teaching methods are used rather than no teaching (which would be a negative control) and comparing this to a new teaching method (experimental condition).

Power analysis A statistical analysis used to check that your sample size will be big enough to detect an effect, so you avoid a type II error.

Primary data Data which comes from tests that you insert directly into your research.

p-value Probability value – that is, the probability that the result may have occurred by chance (e.g. $p = 0.001$ – a 1 in 1,000 probability that the result may have happened by chance). Also known as the significance level.

Q

Qualitative research Research using methods that provide information about the 'human' or personal side of the issue being investigated – for example, information about beliefs, opinions and subjective responses to situations. It typically employs open-ended questions in semi-structured interviews.

Quantitative research Research with fixed scales, closed questions and factors that can be objectively measured, such as body temperature. These data exist as numbers, allowing complex statistical analysis.

Quasi-experiment A study in which it is not possible to manipulate the independent variable or allocate to different conditions, and therefore it compares existing groups. A quasi-experiment could be a non-randomised controlled trial in which a control group is chosen by the researcher because it is similar to the intervention group, or it could be the type of design which compares naturally occurring groups (e.g. boys versus girls, high ability versus low ability pupils). In this second form, both groups are usually exposed to the same treatment

R

Randomisation The process of using random allocation or random sampling.

Random allocation When you use a random process to allocate people to different conditions (in a between-participant design) or to the order in which they experience all the conditions (in a within-participant design).

Random sampling When you use a random process to select the participants you will use in your study in the first place.

Randomised controlled trial (RCT) A piece of research is classed as a randomised controlled trial if it has the following two features. Firstly, the researcher has assigned people to conditions (or levels of the IV), one of which must be a control condition. Secondly, participants are then either randomly allocated to the condition to which they are to be exposed (in a between-participant/matched pairs design) or to the order in which they experience all of the conditions (within-participant design).

Range The distance from your lowest to highest score in a data set. Used as the measure of dispersion if your data is not normally distributed and does not in any way represent a bell curve.

Research aim A formal statement of your research question from which you build a hypothesis.

Research protocol A detailed plan that can act as a manual for yourself and other people who are involved in implementing your research.

S

Secondary data Data that has already been collected prior to you designing a study that makes use of it.

Significance The probability that a change in score may have occurred by chance. A threshold for significance (alpha) is set at the start of a piece of research. This is never less stringent than 0.05, but a more challenging (lower) level (e.g. 0.01) can be chosen if the study is invasive or potentially harmful to any degree. Different authors offer different levels of definition with regard to this concept, depending on the statistical depth the author wishes to include. The American Psychological Association's online glossary defines 'a significant difference' as 'a difference between experimental groups or conditions that would have occurred by chance less than an accepted criterion; in psychology, the criterion most often used is a probability of less than 5 times out of 100, or $p < .05$.'[1]

Standard deviation (SD) A measure of dispersion that tells you how spread out your scores are, assuming they are in some way bell curved and symmetrical.

Standard error of the mean (SEM) A measure that tells you how reliable your mean is.

Surrogate measure. A surrogate measure (or outcome) is one that is a proxy for the real area of interest. For example, if you were researching a general leadership approach, testing maths attainment would be a surrogate form of measurement because the outcome of interest is actually leadership behaviour – an area that might be better measured with a behavioural assessment. Sometimes surrogate outcomes may be the only thing that can be measured. Other times they can be helpful, especially if used in conjunction with assessments that directly relate to the outcome of interest.

T

Test statistic If you use good software packages to analyse your data they will produce a number of values. One of these will be the test statistic. Depending on which test you used the test statistic will usually be either: t, F, Z, U or χ^2 (chi-squared). In the case of the independent samples t-test it will be something like $t = 3.24$. The test statistic tells you the amount of change that has taken place but only for your particular test. Combined with the degrees of freedom for your data (also produced) the software will then calculate the p-value. You need to know about test statistics because most journal articles will expect you to report them alongside the degrees of freedom and p-value. See Brain Box 7.2 (page 132) for more discussion and reporting examples. You can also calculate effect sizes from the test statistic.

Two-tailed hypothesis see **bidirectional hypothesis.**

Type I error Reporting that you have found an effect when it is not really there.

Type II error Reporting that you have not found an effect when it is really there.

V

Variable Something which varies and, in the case of quantitative research, can be counted in some way.

W

Within-participant design The type of research design in which all participants experience all of the conditions. Also known as a within-subject, repeated measures or cross-over design.

---

1   See http://www.apa.org/research/action/glossary. aspx.